'The author's profound sophisticated knowledge of contemporary psychoanalytic . . . and his enormous experience with child and parental conflicts, with a simple and clear, common sense, non-categorical style of parental consultation, without any psychoanalytic terminology or prescriptive affirmations. This approach differs from the usual "how to improve things" texts by appreciating parental willingness to insight in procedures that clearly lead to proven failure, stimulating parental curiosity why things don't work out, and, in the process, motivating them to reach for new understanding.'

Otto F. Kernberg, M.D., *Professor Emeritus,*
Weill Cornell Medical College; Training and
Supervising Analyst, Columbia University
Psychoanalytic Center for Training and Research

.

Understanding Your Child Beyond Words

Understanding Your Child Beyond Words: Psychoanalytic Techniques for Parents will help you unlock a deeper knowledge of your child's feelings, inviting you to explore the deepest questions about parenting and find meaningful answers.

In this book, expert psychoanalyst Cayetano García-Castrillón Armengou teaches you how to look beyond your child's spoken and non-verbal behavior to truly listen to them. By adopting the methods explored in the book, you will become open to new ideas on how to talk, act, and guide your child more effectively. This understanding will help your family grow together, avoid common misunderstandings, and create lasting, meaningful relationships. The book uses simple language and offers numerous examples from everyday reality, showing how everyone in the family can get to know each other better.

Whether your child is already in therapy, you're considering it, or you simply want to enhance your parenting approach, this book provides invaluable insights and guidance to help you unlock your family's full potential.

Cayetano García-Castrillón Armengou is a psychiatrist and psychoanalyst based in Seville, Spain. He is a training and supervising psychoanalyst of the Spanish Society of Psychoanalysis, a member of the Psychoanalytic Association of Madrid and the International Psychoanalytical Association (IPA).

Understanding Your Child Beyond Words

Psychoanalytic Techniques for Parents

Cayetano García-Castrillón Armengou

Routledge
Taylor & Francis Group

LONDON AND NEW YORK

First published in English 2026 by Routledge

Designed cover image: Getty Images
First published 2026
by Routledge
4 Park Square, Milton Park, Abingdon, Oxon OX14 4RN

and by Routledge
605 Third Avenue, New York, NY 10158

Routledge is an imprint of the Taylor & Francis Group, an informa business

Translated by Cheryl Walker

Trademark notice: Product or corporate names may be trademarks or registered trademarks, and are used only for identification and explanation without intent to infringe.

Si no me conoces, no me inventes: Psicoanálisis para padres (Psicoterapias), Published in Spanish by Ediciones Octaedro; 1st edition (1 May 2022)

British Library Cataloguing-in-Publication Data
A catalogue record for this book is available from the British Library

ISBN: 978-1-032-94742-6 (hbk)
ISBN: 978-1-032-94741-9 (pbk)
ISBN: 978-1-003-58154-3 (ebk)

DOI: 10.4324/9781003581543

Typeset in Times New Roman
by Apex CoVantage, LLC

Contents

About the contributors

Co-authors and contributors:

Frank García-Castrillón Armengou, PhD, is a clinical psychologist and professor at the International University of La Rioja, Spain.

Blanca García-Castrillón Fernández is a primary school teacher and graduated from the CEU San Pablo University, Seville, Spain.

Acknowledgments

I would like to express my gratitude to my family, Lucia Pablo and Blanca, and my sister, Martha, for their support in the making of this book. I am enormously grateful to my psychoanalytic professors, Dr. Eulalia Torras de Beá, Dr. Victor Hernadez Espinosa, Dr. Jose Luis Lillo, and Mrs. Nuria Abelló de Bofill (Spanish Society of Psychoanalysis members, SEP, IPA), who taught me so much about babies, children, adolescents, and families. To my father, Dr. Cayetano García-Castrillón de la Rosa, to whom I owe so many things, among them, having dedicated myself to this profession that he loved and was so passionate about. And to my brother, Frank García-Castrillón Armengou, clinical psychologist and professor at the International University of La Rioja, Spain, for his successful contributions. To my colleagues who helped me and still help me to grow, learn, and progress, patiently tolerating my limitations with affection, without whom this book would never have seen the light of day. Dr. Antonio de la Plata Caballero and Rosa Royo Esqués (members SEP- IPA) for their invaluable support. To Mrs. Elina Wechsler, Mr. Daniel Schoffer, and Mrs. Teresa Aguilar Ortuño (Psychoanalytic Association of Madrid members, APM-IPA), who have provided me the opportunity to discover and learn more. To Mr. Alfons Icart (SEP-IPA) for the enthusiasm he has always transmitted to me, to *the Fundacion Orienta*- Barcelona, and to the *"Revista de Psicopatologia y Salud Mental del niño y del adolescente."* To Mr. Xavier Costa for his unconditional support of this project. And I also appreciate Andy Cohen (psychoanalyst in training of the South African Psychoanalytic Association) for his encouraging contributions to improving the book. I would also like to thank Professor Otto Kernberg, MD, for his generosity and kindness in having written the prologue of the book. All of them have accompanied and encouraged me during the book's long *"gestation"* process and, of course, to all the families who have continually taught me over the years.

Dr. Cayetano García-Castrillón Armengou

Preface

The present volume is an outstanding, original approach to helping troubled parents to deal with troublesome, chronic interactional difficulties with their children from the earliest years through late adolescence. It combines the author's profound, sophisticated knowledge of contemporary psychoanalytic theory and practice and his enormous experience with child and parental conflicts with a simple and clear, common sense, non-categorical style of parental consultation, without any psychoanalytic terminology or prescriptive affirmations. This approach differs from the usual *"how to improve things"* texts by appreciating parental willingness to insight into procedures that clearly lead to proven failure, stimulating parental curiosity about why things don't work out, and, in the process, motivating them to reach for a new understanding of what goes on in their child's mind and in their own experience in good and bad moments.

What seems an ordinary, free-floating musing turns out to lead to illuminating observations and effective changes in understanding and action, in which the experienced psychoanalyst would recognize the efforts of an accurate interpretation. In establishing the conditions for a new interest that parents and their children may develop in what happens in each other in their confrontations—yes, parents will learn to introspect, a new family orientation is fostered, and past and present of both parents and children are looked at in new, previously unsuspected ways.

Brief summaries of dominant conflicts and their management and a few chapters providing a broader approach to psychological development are presented in daily language that is easily understood in the context of the author's style of engagement. This book is a learning and growing experience for both parents and children and a most needed and welcome help for psychoanalysts and psychodynamically oriented psychotherapists of children and adolescents who must deal with the parental environments of their patients. And it should be a delight for any intellectually inclined person interested in the age in which so much develops, for good (and for bad).

Otto F. Kernberg, M.D.
Professor Emeritus, Weill Cornell Medical College.
Training and Supervising Analyst,
Columbia University Psychoanalytic
Center for Training and Research

Author's note

In this book, I have used the terms *"mom"* and *"dad"* to refer to parental figures in the clinical examples and reflections presented. I want to emphasize that my intention is not to overlook or oversimplify the richness of modern family configurations, including those where both parents are of the same gender.

It is important to clarify that, beyond the gender of the caregivers, what truly matters are the maternal and paternal functions that each parental figure can fulfill. These functions are not tied to gender but are instead related to the roles of care, protection, emotional support, and guidance that all parents—regardless of their gender identity—carry out in their children's lives. Even in single-parent families, the caregiver naturally flows between both maternal and paternal functions to meet their child's needs.

For simplicity and readability, I have chosen to use the terms *"mom"* and *"dad"* throughout the book. I trust and hope that readers will understand this decision as a practical choice to make the text easier to follow rather than an attempt to exclude or ignore the diversity of modern family structures.

Thank you for your openness and for joining me in this exploration toward more conscious and empathetic parenting.

Cayetano García-Castrillón Armengou, MD

Part I

The journey into parenthood

Chapter 1

Introduction

Cayetano García-Castrillón Armengou

From the moment a baby is born, parents endeavor with all their strength and abilities to ensure everything goes well. Parents dedicate countless hours to improving their family and their children. So, if the baby cries, they will want to know what is wrong. Why is he crying? What is the cause: is it hunger, pain, fear, etc.? If they are overly worried, they will seek help, get information from various sources, go to professionals, etc. With this book, I intend to contribute ideas that will provide parents with more information and the possibility of understanding more aspects of their children. In fact, attending to the natural curiosity of parents to know more propels the development of their children.

By going beyond words and behaviors and actively listening to their children, parents will be able to connect with their children, discovering and embracing their child's true self, getting new ideas about how to proceed, how to talk, how to act, and how to guide their children more effectively. And thus, avoid impulsive management of emotions and conflicts, because this is doomed to failure.

This will let parents reduce conflicts, raising confidence and strengthen their bonds with their child. And avoid missing out on the enormous potential for help that parents can provide to their children and that they will be grateful for.

However, it took me quite a while to decide to write this book. Even now, I am not yet clear about the reason for the apparent delay. Still, I sense it is difficult for me to address parents *"openly"* without knowing what personal and family circumstances shape their lives and their ideas of parenthood. In addition, each child's particularities and innumerable circumstances of all kinds influence the course of child-rearing and family life, making each family a different and

DOI: 10.4324/9781003581543-2

unique space and place. No two families are alike, at least not the ones I have had the chance to meet, and I hope I have helped.

Consequently, this observation leads me to recommend that those who read this book do so from a critical standpoint and not as a definitive guide or as a dogmatic record of right and wrong.

What encouraged me to write this book was my observation of the difficulties of the parents I counseled in understanding their children and of the children in getting to know and better understand their parents. I sometimes think that my work as a psychoanalyst and psychiatrist has focused mainly on helping them to *"get to know each other better,"* after which many misunderstandings, quarrels, mistrust, and resentments seemed to disappear as if by magic. Well, *"magic"* after weeks, or sometimes months, of working with parents through distressing and challenging times.

To me, parents asking for help seems like one of the most complex decisions. It's very painful to admit that things aren't going well. Feelings of failure often invade parents and make them feel so guilty that their guilt does not allow them to seek help. Many believe they will be accused of being bad parents if they seek help. Nothing could be further from the truth.

On other occasions, it sparks a repeated symphony of mutual recriminations by the parents that not only doesn't fix anything but often ends in a rift in the couple or in singling out the child as the only cause of the conflicts. Which also does not help much. Let's not forget that, many times, intense feelings of guilt translate into an outpouring of reproaches. It also occurs due to ignorance.

But those who have been able to overcome this difficulty, which is the norm, take a giant step, perhaps without knowing to what extent things can be fixed. If there is a feeling that describes how parents first come to the consultation, it is that of profound hopelessness. That is, with a lot of suffering, impotence, and pain. So, parents have it bad, unbelievably bad. But sometimes, given the anguish caused by difficulties *"with the children"* or *"of the children,"* hastiness makes it involuntarily challenging to seek help. If there is one thing that people want to eliminate as soon as possible, it is distress. However, in general, the maneuvers to quickly get rid of distress increase it because we act more by impulses than by as calm a deliberation as *"possible"* based on what is *"possible."* This hastiness will prevent us from gaining a more profound understanding of what is happening, what is truly going on with our child, and the potential for assistance that we parents can have. In addition, it can lead us to *"the tendency"* to *"invent"* the other person. Let's see a situation that reflects how easy it is to imagine (and to make up the other person) without knowledge of them or the situation. This opens the way for a new paradigm of parenting that I call: *"Rethinking Parenting."*

If you don't know me, don't make me up

It is as follows. I was in the gym exercising, and in front of me were three ladies on stationary bikes chatting loud enough for everyone around them to hear what they were talking about. Their discussion goes as follows:

Mrs. 1. (in front of me on the right): *"Look at X's parents."*
Mrs. 2. (in the center): *"He was held back last year."*
Mrs. 1. *"Well, they are throwing a party for him."*
Mrs. 3. (in front of me on the left): *"Despite repeating the year, he still failed two subjects . . . and are they going to have a party?"*

Almost in unison, the three commented, *"How outrageous!"* I also thought it was outrageous, and that child had not earned a party. My first impulse was to agree with the ladies, so I was Mrs. 4, thinking like them. My head was like the one in the drawing in Figure 1.1.

An empty head that only contained what I had heard, nothing more, no elaboration, not knowing anything. That is, if one does not know the circumstances, events, situations, etc., one runs the significant risk of making up the predicament (and worse, the viable solutions) without really knowing anything. If both the professional and the parents remain at that point, we can do little to help get out of difficulties. We will enter the path of accusation and blame under supposed knowledge, leading us irretrievably into error. If we do not know or understand, we will fabricate, if not everything, too much. We are moving further and further away from the possibility of really knowing what may be going on. What could be happening then in this case, of which I knew nothing? Let's look at different possibilities that should at least be considered to rule them out or not. Some possible hypotheses could be:

1. What if the boy has been hospitalized for four months, has tried hard, and *"only"* has two subjects left? In this case, would the boy deserve a party? That would change everything, wouldn't it?

Figure 1.1 This drawing is by a 9-year-old girl who draws herself without a brain.

More possibilities:

2. What if parents feel *"bad"* and have to show themselves as *"good"* by giving the party? What if they blame themselves for their child's failure and have to celebrate a failure to alleviate their guilt?
3. What if the parents are trying to *"de-dramatize"* the situation and, instead of accusing, celebrate the child's progress compared to the previous year's results?
4. What if parents have realized that pushing and demanding too much is not good and are trying to change by decreasing the level of demands on the child?
5. And if the child is depressed and has some problem in class, other students hit him, make fun of him, and he has not been able to tell his parents, and the parents have detected his sadness and try to encourage him with the party?

Any of these hypotheses are *"possible,"* and surely there are more. It is clear, at least, that before judging and condemning, it is advisable to know and obtain as much information as possible.

From my point of view, it is crucial to know that taking for granted without knowledge is common in some situations we may encounter. For example, when we lack sufficient information, we are very shocked (distressed) by what our children show us, or even if our pride blinds us. I think we need to be vigilant about the risk of becoming simple-minded, inquisitorial, and finally getting very lost. One of the purposes of this book is to avoid this risk. But it's not easy to realize that we don't know as much as we think, and sometimes, it's because we simply forget to ask.

We simply forget to ask

Let's look at another example:

At a lecture I gave at a school to about 200 parents of teenage boys, the most frequent questions used to be, *"How long should you let them use the cell phone?"*, *"How to respond to failing grades?"*, *"How do you get teenagers to clean and straighten their room?"* The parents, overwhelmed by these issues, took advantage of my presence, searching for the definitive prescription to reach an end-point that would immediately resolve the tensions that these situations generated in the day-to-day lives of the families.

At that lecture, it was evident from the different statements by parents, along the lines of, *"What would become of their children tomorrow if they continued down that (wrong) path?"* that they were generally terrified for their children's future and considered these questions as the *"future meter."* They were repeatedly stuck on these questions without being able to consider much more. In the face of all that worry, I asked them if they remembered when they were teenagers and how they saw things then.

This question gave rise, in quite a lot of them, to the observation and realization that their children acted remarkably similar to what they did. This realization led to an interesting debate. It also allowed us to talk about de-dramatizing things a bit to tone them down at home. With this discussion, I clarified that, in my opinion, we are so worried that the boys will ruin their future, which causes us to forget that when we were teenagers, we were going through the same thing as them and that we have all pulled through in the end. Also, I reminded them that adolescence is as tumultuous for their boys as it was for us in our day. Finally, we came to the conclusion that it is very difficult for us to see the advances, the achievements of the boys, the positive things, the challenges they face, what their friend group means to them, the hookups, how nervous they get in the face of all these new challenges, as it happened to us. Some even acknowledged, *"I was much worse than my son."*

Interestingly, many parents commented on how they would have liked their parents (currently grandparents) to have responded and acted differently in their day when they were teenagers and what they would have changed. Others say that, in reality, this is forgotten, and we repeat what we once criticized about our own parents when it came to us being *"the teenager at home."* It was a fascinating debate that paved the way for modification and in which more than one parent ended up saying that it would be good to listen more to the children because they would have loved to be *"listened to more."* I told them I found this an excellent conclusion and encouraged them to do so.

As you can see, there was a turning point in the talk. Based on the questions about what to do, the conclusion was that more listening was needed. And, in my opinion, listening attentively to children is one of the things that most help us to know them thoroughly. Another observation that these parents contributed was that, before, the fathers spoke little with the children, and everything remained in the hands of the mothers. They argued that the father's role in raising the children was totally missing. Today, fortunately, this old premise is being dispelled.

I explained to them that, in my daily work with adolescents and children, they often tell me that their parents do not understand anything and that *"they always say the same thing."* Many say it in an apparent criticism of their parents, but in all of them, one notices that deep down, they want to talk to their parents more, and I think that many times, children do not know how to create the conditions to do it, because a teenager feels *infantile* if he does. That identification with being childish restrains them a lot, which is why they often do not facilitate dialogue. They confuse us greatly and even make us believe that they are not interested in talking to us. Well, nothing is further from reality, but they recognize that desire openly, which during childhood is easy, is very difficult in adolescence.

That's why we find that when our children enter adolescence, they talk less to us, and, in some ways, which displeases us. But the desire in them continues, even if they tell us, *"Don't ask me,"* *"You are annoying,"* or *"Leave me alone."* I think that these answers must be relativized because, if we do not, we run the risk of not asking them questions. In addition, they usually choose the time to talk. After these clarifications, I commented that I usually tell teenagers that they can make their parents understand better by talking to them more, by not systematically blaming them and that their parents, deep down, are human and cannot figure out everything (many are surprised when they take the step and confirm that their parents pay attention to them). The second issue is that it is quite easy for us to forget to ask them how they are or how life is going. I also took the opportunity to ask the parents when, in the last month, they had asked their children how life was going. And to raise their hand if they asked that question.

Not one parent raised their hand. Surprising, isn't it, or not so surprising? Let's have a look. Were all parents disinterested in their children? Obviously not. I explained that the stress, the hurry, the cleanliness of the room, the cell phone, and the grades worry us so much that we sometimes stop seeing the essentials. Not absent was the mother or father who *"reminded me"* that, when asked, the response of the adolescent son has been limited to an *"I'm fine,"* settling the question with a single stroke. I also explained to them that, from a young age, it is worthwhile that we get used to asking children how they are and if they are worried about anything to make it common for these issues to be part of the family dialogue. This is a good family vaccine. And what does this vaccine protect against? It protects us from entering the spiral of mistrust.

Finally, I explained to them that no child I have treated has refused to talk to their parents. Some (quite a few) even tell me, *"You can tell my parents everything,"* and most say that I can say *"almost everything,"* usually leaving out the topic of their dating relationships. The younger ones are always happy to talk to their parents. It is clear that no treatment of children with difficulties should exclude the parents. Teenagers have never said no to treatment when I have explained that I will frequently talk with their parents about situations because, in addition to being their parents, they are also people who are interested in them, who are suffering like them, and that excluding them would be a serious mistake. To date, no teenager, including those who seemingly disown their parents, has told me not to talk to them.

We cannot forget that, in one way or another, every adolescent feels that they no longer have those parents (idealized in childhood) available, who were there for everything, whom they considered infallible, and their protectors. They are left without those parents, and they are the ones who will have to start managing on their own. This realization, unconsciously, makes most of them angry, and at the same time, they miss them. Any relationship with parents will undergo a complex *"reset"* process for everyone during adolescence, but not only during adolescence. Let's see an example:

"The reset" process: starting over with fresh eyes

However, it is not only in adolescence that this reset takes place; in fact, it is somewhat permanent. Let's look at a brief example. Ana is a young mother who has two daughters. One is three years old, and the other is only six months old. She calls me in distress because her older daughter's behavior is out of control: she is angry, cannot be separated from her mother at night, sleeps in her parents' room, and hits her little sister even though she also loves her very much. She tells me her eldest daughter does not want to be with her father. The young mother tells me, almost in tears, that she can't take it anymore and is overwhelmed. She doesn't want to do a bad job, but when she yells at her daughter, she feels very guilty and like a bad mother.

She doesn't understand why her daughter won't leave her side. On the next visit that the father attended, he commented: *"I think I have a say too."* He seemed upset because he felt relegated to the background. I asked him what he thought of this situation; he told me that he held back but that there were things he disagreed with.

The mother told me that her daughter could not stand the father, and it was impossible for her to be with him. On further inquiry, we discovered that the mother was an only child and that, due to various painful circumstances, she had lost contact with her mother as a child, although not completely. Both the parents and I wondered if she might be concerned that her daughter, at the slightest separation, would feel that her mother was quite distant from her, even if she was with her father, and that the mother might be concerned that her daughter would be as hurt as she was by the accidental estrangement from her mother in her childhood. This revelation turned out to be an amusing moment in the interview as the mother, laughing, said, *"I knew I was the one who didn't want her to pull away."*

This mother felt that her daughter would blame her for the slightest distancing, perhaps in a clear re-staging of her discomfort with her mother's estrangement.

We talked about how this made her feel like a bad mother, the mother who fails if she distances herself, the mother who would also fail if she gave the dad room, etc., fearing to cause her daughter to be angry with her.

In reality, there was some truth in all this. The birth of a baby sister made the mother withdraw somewhat, but to withdraw is not to abandon. When we could articulate this issue, we decided to explain to the older daughter that having a little sister did not mean being without mom, and that, although she is with the baby, she is also very present with her and that if the daughter goes with daddy, her mother will be very happy to see her when she comes back and to discover how much fun she has had with daddy. Furthermore, she could then play with her little sister. Here, another nice moment came up when I told the mother not only to tell her older daughter this but also herself.

Here, we can see the desire of these parents to know, to be curious, and to understand. This mother had made a mess of herself; she mixed up distancing with abandonment, and it was she who then feared separation from her baby.

They understood this quickly. After these explanations, we thought of some ideas that could come in handy. I list the most relevant one: that they explain to their daughter that mom is busy with the baby sister but that it doesn't mean she doesn't love her, that she still loves her. And that daddy will be with her.

The beginning of the following interview was very striking. It started with these comments from the parents, *"The impossible has happened. She has been with her father non-stop and has had an enjoyable time. We had a fun time."* I commented that they looked happy about the achievement. It was a great relief for this mother to see that her daughter did not get angry when she was away from her. Perhaps this mother was very grieved with her mother at the time, although today, they have an acceptable relationship despite the unfortunate difficulties they experienced.

Reference list

Blum, H. P. (2004). Separation-individuation theory and attachment theory. *Journal of the American Psychoanalytic Association*, 52(2):535–553.

Britton, R. (1998). Subjectivity, objectivity, and potential space. In *Belief and imagination*. Routledge.

Britton, R. (2004). Subjectivity, objectivity, and triangular space. *The Psychoanalytic Quarterly*, 73:47–61.

García-Castrillón, C. (2007). *Ser padres, ¿una misión imposible?* Ed. Glosa.

Schoffer, D. (2008). *La Función Paterna en la Clínica Freudiana*. Lugar Editorial.

Schultheis, A. M., Mayes, L. C., and Rutherford, H. J. V. (2019). Associations between emotion regulation and parental reflective functioning. *Journal of Child and Family Studies*, 28:1094–1104.

Winnicott, D. (1958). The capacity to be alone. *The International Journal of Psychoanalysis*, 39:416.

Winnicott, D. (1965). *Los procesos de maduración y el ambiente facilitador*. Buenos Aires: Paidós.

Chapter 2

Becoming mom and dad

Cayetano García-Castrillón Armengou

Introduction: a transformative journey

One of the most relevant issues when it comes to being parents is that, since we know we are going to be, we imagine what our child will be like, or rather, how we would like them to be. Regarding names, one of the few things we can choose because we will have to accept the others, for example, sex. In some cases, it is already a competition for a name that pleases the father or the mother, a name that is a posthumous tribute to some beloved, departed relative, or a name that by *"family tradition"* comes next, which leaves little room to maneuver, lest we face disappointment if we stop complying with the *"tradition."* Or we pick the names we like, period.

As soon as the baby is born, we will give them more names in the form of adjectives, depending on how we see their personality; thus, if the baby is a big eater, we will call them *"greedy,"* or if they are active, *"the live wire,"* etc. These qualifiers will shape the baby's personality, a personality that will be a discovery for the parents. That is to say, our desire to know and learn about them is there, the fruit of our great curiosity as parents, even before they are born. Our baby will give us that new and undaunted status: that of being fathers and mothers. But there is another way to get to know our babies: intuition.

Afterward, we will have almost the entire family trying to find similarities in the baby. Thus, some will say it has the father's nose, the grandfather's hands, and, of course, so-and-so's chin—a classic. If we notice, we all try to identify and see something in the baby that is familiar to us. We have to get to know and give a *"personality"* to our new and unknown family members.

DOI: 10.4324/9781003581543-3

A little later, the grandparents' comments, above all, will help us even to see aspects of ourselves. For example, when grandparents comment and reminisce that the now-parents were also babies: *"As a baby you were . . . ," "I remember that one day you . . . "* In other words, there was a time when we were also babies, children, and adolescents. Periods of which we remember little or nothing, but we were. And frequently, we begin to see how much our fathers and mothers did for us.

If we already have experience, when a second baby is born, we will immediately realize how different it is from the first. It reacts differently and responds differently, and its motor activity is not the same. So, we see that they are entirely different and that what worked for one does not work for the other. In other words, we have to reinvent ourselves as parents, adapt to the new baby's personality, and draw on our experience. We will no longer worry so much about cleaning the pacifier if it falls, we will no longer sterilize it, nor will we be alarmed if the baby does not eat absolutely everything. Yes, we will be a little calmer unless we want everything to happen the same way, forgetting that everyone *"is how he is, even babies."*

A baby's world: What we learn from observing their world

Let's look at an example based on the observation of a baby[1] I conducted on March 10, many years ago. The baby was two months and five days old:

I arrive at the appointed time, 11 in the morning. I find the baby and his mother in the yard, and the mother says, *"He's been awake since 8 a.m. and hasn't slept. Yesterday, I took him to the pediatrician. He has a runny nose, and he has vomited the entire 10 a.m. bottle, so there is the poor little guy—and I am a disaster with the nose drops, and he doesn't like it when I use the bulb syringe to remove the snot, poor thing—he's having a hard time, and I am worse. We're having a terrible time."* Then she tells the baby: *"Look, Cayetano has arrived,"* and the baby looks at me. I have the impression that he already knows me. *"He's pleasant this week; he's very appreciative . . . . The others didn't do that. The smiles he gives me It's curious how one forgets from one child to the next—I didn't even know how to pick him up when he was born—now I do—it's been such a long time."* The baby cannot breathe, so the mother sits him up and kisses him on the nose. The baby is comforted (me too), and she says in his ear, *"What a pain this cold is."* Then, the mom gets up and tells me she's going for the droplets and (for the first time) gives me the baby. I tell the baby, *"You're sick!"* And he smiles at me. The mother arrives, gives him the drops, and he calms down. The mother asks me, *"Does he look bigger to you?"* I say *yes*; he seems to grow from one week to the next. She leaves him in the crib, and he begins to cry, so she takes him in her arms and sings to him and, at the same time, says to the baby: *"I'm still a little embarrassed to sing to you in front of Cayetano."*

She then asks me if I know of a store called Noah's Ark. I say no, and she tells me she loves it. *"I like it because, even if you go to buy something as small as a screw, they take care of you, even if the other customers have to wait, they take out 50 screws—what patience they have!—but one comes out of there relaxed. I buy threads for cross stitching."* After a while, she gives the baby a bottle, saying, *"It's not time, but he will be hungry; I will not give him much, just in case. Do you think he will be cold?"* I reply that I don't think so. The mom urges him to take the bottle, but he refuses it. She affectionately says, *"My baby doesn't want more."* She doesn't insist anymore. The baby poops, she changes his diaper, puts him in the crib, and he goes to sleep. We all seem to *"breathe"* easier. She tells me that the dad gives him the pacifier when he drops it because otherwise, he sucks his thumb; she also tells me that the cross-stitch is because she is making him a washcloth with a little cow, which has turned out very ugly, and that the balloon is missing. As I leave, she reminds me about the store and says it is a good place. I thank her for the advice.

Obviously, at the store, they have the same calmness and patience that she has with her baby and that he is so grateful for, from which we can extract some ideas to behave with our babies:

1. How vital patience is, not telling the mother *"what to do."* It's easy to see how they are getting to know each other, understand each other, and face the first little cold of the cute baby's life.
2. I was struck by the mother's reference to the time and patience that the shopkeeper gave her, even when she bought the most minor thing. This aspect can be extended to the relationship with the children. Babies and children gratefully receive the offering of time

and dedication that creates an exclusive connection, even in the smallest details.

3. The previous assertion disproves many parents' pervasive ideas and concerns that the baby will get used to being held and that they want to control the relationship. Nothing could be further from the truth. Babies are not fussy (we adults tend to be much more so than they are). Another thing is that sometimes we don't understand what is happening to them. So, the more they are held, the better; little by little, they will acquire more autonomy and more curiosity about the world around them. No baby has ever become *"glued"* to a few arms. Only when a baby has had the security of having been welcomed will they be able to detach, little by little, with greater security and confidence.

4. The importance of parental intuition is evident. Intuition often makes it possible to identify what babies cannot verbalize. If this intuition is accompanied by flexibility, the chances of detecting where things are going increase significantly. On one occasion, at another meeting with parents, a mother was there with her baby in the stroller. As I was talking, I noticed the mother looking a little nervous. It seemed to me that she was worried that the baby would wake up, cry, and interfere with the conference. The mother repeatedly got up to put the pacifier in the baby's mouth. I turned to her to tell her that if she was worried about coming with her baby, I didn't mind. I jokingly told her that her baby was the youngest attendee ever at one of my conferences. The mother relaxed, and I asked her, *"How do you know how your baby is doing?"* The mother gave a sweet answer, *"It depends on whether he smiles or not. My feelings help, I think. Is that right, Doctor?"* As you can imagine, my answer was: *"Yes. They are very helpful, and your baby is fortunate to have such a sensitive mother with him."*

Observation as a neutralizer of idealization

So, from birth, we are shaping, observing, and defining our child's personality. Then, as the baby grows, they will provide us with more information in several ways and on an ongoing basis.

However, we sometimes look for the child we do not have (a unique and idealized model). We look for the *"ideal"* son or daughter. This leaves us without the capacity to observe. This is a serious problem because, if we are unaware of it, we will exaggerate the demands over the child. The child's experience is that they constantly disappoint their parents, who will love them less, and their personal security, along with the (basic) assurance of being loved and, therefore, having their needs met, vanishes. They are frightened children, afraid to show their curiosity, try, and experiment; they withdraw from the threat they feel of not being loved when they see that their parents are rarely happy with them. This situation is challenging and painful. But, sometimes, we do it thinking that things will turn out well this way. This is often evident when parents constantly compare their children with others. On one occasion, a teenager told me: *"It is clear that my parents would have preferred another child, not me. They really like my cousin."*

In conclusion, I would highlight that the more observational capacity is enhanced in parents, the more perspective they will have concerning their children and themselves. In addition, the more you observe, the more curious you are.

Note

1 *"Baby Observation"* is a seminar that takes place in the process of training as an IPA psychoanalyst and in other disciplines, which consists of *"observing"* the relationship between the baby, its mother, and the environment during the first year of life. Observation takes place weekly.

Bibliography

Bick, E., and Harris, M. (2018). *The Tavistock model: Collected papers of Martha Harris and Esther Bick.* Karnac Books.

Fairbairn, W. (1946). Object-relationships and dynamic structure. *The International Journal of Psychoanalysis*, 27:30.

Fonagy, P., and Target, M. (2002). Jugando con la realidad III. In *Libro anual de psicoanálisis XVI*. São Paulo-Brasil: Ed. Escuta Ltda.

Furman, E. (1995). Working with and through the parents. *Child Analysis: Clinical, Theoretical and Applied*, 6:21–42.

Furman, E. (1999). The impact of parental interventions. *International Journal of Psychoanalysis*, 80:172.

Spitz, R. (1965). *The first tear of life*. New York, NY: International University Press.

Chapter 3

Son, you make it so difficult

The mystery of temporary deafness

Cayetano García-Castrillón Armengou

It is evident that listening to children is particularly important. But when a child is causing us enormous strain, or when the problems they are causing may not allow us to detect the importance of what they are telling us, it isn't easy to listen to them. What they usually *"unleash"* in those moments of tension are key comments since, in a way, they tell us what is happening to them. But since they manage to irritate or upset us, as I said, it is quite common for us to overlook it.

This is not dire because they will undoubtedly repeat it again and again. Recognizing this phenomenon, which I call *"temporary deafness,"* can help us to detect these stray comments of enormous importance. Comments such as *"I don't love you," "I hate you,"* and *"Leave me alone"* are like the thread that sticks out of the skein that we can pull on. It is not uncommon to hear children who *"cause trouble"* at home say that their parents don't love them. It surprises me even more to see how children can perfectly detect how their parents are doing emotionally. When I tell parents, they often say, *"How do they know if we haven't said anything?"* I reply that not everything is said or transmitted with words.

Let's look at an example of how children end up unleashing *"everything."*

Why a little sister? Understanding family dynamics

This time, I was at a conference for parents of young children. During the parent question and answer section, a mother remarked that her daughter exhibits constant, ongoing, appalling jealousy and that she has been hitting her sister since she was born. The mother, clearly

DOI: 10.4324/9781003581543-4

desperate, told me that although she had said to her that they loved her very much and that she was hurting the little sister, she observed that the child could not control her jealous impulses. The (reasonable) punishments did not have the desired effect either. And as happens on so many other occasions, the mother told me, *"I have run out of punishments,"* adding that, until the birth of the little sister, her daughter was *"normal,"* but that now she seems to be *"possessed."* This made her incredibly sad, and it hurt her to see all this suffering.

I thought about it and told her that I had the impression that her daughter had understood that the new baby was an attack against her and that she didn't understand why they had brought another baby. And just as she had experienced it as an attack, she responded *"in kind."* She possibly felt that her parents were unhappy with her, leading them to look for another baby they liked better. I made it clear to her that, inevitably, the arrival of a sibling means many things, and among them, that the new baby will take center stage or, at the very least, the attention will be divided. Each child interprets this in their own way; therefore, what I was saying was a *"viable"* possibility. After all, if a child understands their parents are happy with them, why do they need another one? Or are they not that happy? Typically, any child who is going to have a sibling is looking for explanations. And if we pay attention, they will eventually bring them to light.

Following these comments, the mother said that the daughter had asked her, *"Why did you bring that baby?"* and added, *"You didn't ask my permission!"*

I told the mother that they were in a vicious circle because if the older one hit her sister, she was the *"bad"* one, confirming that the other was the *"good"* one. The mother replied that the little one was particularly good. I recommended the mother talk to the daughter and make it clear to her that her little sister did not come because they were not happy with her but because they wanted another child as much as they had wanted to have her. And that if they were paying more attention to her sister, it is because she needs it, unlike her, who is older, and that they appreciate that very much because they enjoy things with her that they cannot yet enjoy with the little sister.

These reactions are generally triggered when the new baby is no longer a baby: when they walk, they are more communicative and are more active with their development and growth. For many *"older siblings,"* at that moment, they are already a serious threat. Afterward, we talked about how to prepare a child for the arrival of a baby brother or sister and how to support him or her through the change: this was thanks to the determined willingness of this mother to talk about her situation.

How fear shapes relationships and behaviors

Support is of utmost importance, as Freud describes in the following anecdote from lecture 25, which dealt with anxiety. It is as follows: Freud listened from a neighbor's room to a child afraid of the dark. This is the conversation Freud heard: *"Auntie, talk to me, I'm afraid."* To which the aunt replies, *"What good is it to you if you can't see me?"* The boy replies, *"There is a lighter feeling when someone talks."* After this, Freud comments that longing in the dark is transformed into anxiety. So, with the voice, the yearning dissipates, and the fear disappears. This boy was not asking for an explanation of the fear; he was simply pointing out that by speaking, the fear diminished. Thus, providing support in the darkness, from ignorance and uncertainty, is the first step in approaching any conflict confidently and hoping to finally understand what hinders growth, family life, studies, etc. When this is understood, everything becomes easier.

Let's look at another situation:

John and Anne are a couple with three children. Unfortunately, their youngest daughter has severe epilepsy that conditions family life and keeps these parents in constant fear that their daughter's life is in grave danger during seizures. Continuous visits to emergency rooms and doctors to keep the risks of the disease at bay set the tone for the family's life. In the initial interview with them, the mother complained bitterly to her husband about his obsession with her daughter and that he was very controlling. Meanwhile, the father reproached the mother, saying it was the right thing to do because of the illness. In turn, the father lectured the mother that her daughter could not do everything because of the risk she was running, while the mother told him that being hyper-controlling would not reduce the risks. Looks of rebuke and displeasure between them accompanied this repetitive and reiterative dialogue. Occasionally, they pointed out that if this continued, they would separate. Neither of them would give in under any circumstances. And when an epileptic seizure occurred, they blamed each other for what had happened.

At the same time, both were saddened to note that the other children were relegated to the background in everyday life. It pained the parents to have to rely on them to care for their sick sister, and they were concerned about whether their other children's lives would be affected once the parents were absent, in addition to the financial cost to their other children. In a sense, both parents felt guilty.

We can see how these parents were, logically, worried about the present and the future and were living under a continuous threat of death. However, they told me that the prognosis given by the neurologists was two or three years of life at the most. That is to say that his daughter would not reach the age of three. In other words, the countdown was about to begin. Thanks to the admirable effort of these parents and the work of the doctors, survival had been prolonged to more than 20 years. However, it seemed that these parents did not appreciate this outstanding achievement. They were just caught up in disputes. In the interview, each one looked at me as if to say, *"You see how she (he) is,"* looking to me for confirmation.

It seemed that they both demanded that I should agree with them, that I should be the judge. I explained to them what I just mentioned. Their answer was that yes, that's what they thought. They even explained to me that the reason for coming was, verbatim, *"Let's go to a doctor to tell us who is screwing up?"* If we observe closely, they could not think, *"Let's go to the doctor to see what is happening to us or to understand how we are handling this difficult situation."* I also explained this to them. I also told them that if I ultimately played judge, it would come down to determining who the *"winner"* and *"loser"* are, assuming that everything the loser has done has been detrimental to their daughter's health. Furthermore, in the end, the loser would believe I was wrong and had allied myself with one of them and disqualified the other.

After explaining all this, which they understood, I outlined my point of view as follows:

1. I asked them the following question going around in my head. *How was it possible that they were not conscious of or proud of themselves as parents for having achieved the extraordinary survival of their daughter despite having two hugely different ways of approaching the situation?* They were surprised by the question.
2. I told them that it was clear to me that one of them was saying: *"Let the child do whatever she wants and let her live her life,"* and

the other one, *"If I let her be, I put her in vital danger."* This translated into constant reproaches. You are a super-controller, and that is harmful. On the other hand, being super-controlled protects her. This was the duality that had them trapped.

3. I explained to them that I believed they had not realized that these polarized positions and their management in the background were an ongoing search for balance, to find the most reasonable, safest possible point when confronted with the constant threat of the disease. However, in the face of the anguish of feeling and experiencing that, unfortunately, it is not possible to control the risk completely. The fear of the disease made them think there was a unique and definitive way to fully control the danger. This made them understand that the threat was in the other person's position and way of coping, not the illness itself. And that I understood that it is extremely hard to see that her survival cannot be guaranteed.

These comments stopped the initial disputes of the interview and allowed them to appreciate their efforts as parents and that their ongoing management had been successful.

In general, when parents have to undertake a child's disability, they tend toward this polarization in the management mode. On the other hand, mourning begins because all the expectations, family life, family economy, dealings with doctors, and even the parents' important personal and professional sacrifices are going to be affected.

In my experience with children with disabilities, I admire their ability to enjoy the *"little things in life"* and how much they appreciate them. Let me point out that I think many should take note of this.

Concerning what I have just said, I asked these parents if they saw their daughter as happy. They replied that they did. She has social media, she socializes, and she likes to wear makeup. I told them that this is also thanks to them.

Finally, in addition to proposing a follow-up, I gave them a recommendation. It was to talk to their other children about all of this, ask them about their concerns, if they have felt displaced at times, etc. In short, to convey to them that, as parents, they understand that it also has repercussions for them.

Reference list

Balint, M. (1969). Trauma and object relationship. *The International Journal of Psychoanalysis*, 50:429.

Freud, S. (1915). *Considetaciones de actualidad sobre la guerra y la muerte*. Obras Completas, Vol. VI. Amorrortu Editores.

Freud, S. (1937). *Construcciones en psicoanálisis*. Obras Completas de Sigmund Freud, Vol. 23. Ed. Amorrortu.

Icart, A., and Freixas, J. (2013). *La familia: Comprensión dinámica e intervenciones terapéuticas*. Ed. Herder.

Novick, K. K., and Novick, J. (2005). *Working with parents makes therapy work*. Aronson.

Sandler, J. (1967). Trauma, strain and development. In S. S. Furst (ed.), *Psychic trauma*. New York and London: Basic Books.

Chapter 4

The mirror effect
Projecting expectations and experiences

Cayetano García-Castrillón Armengou

Besides our understanding concern as parents that everything goes well, our past is sometimes *"very present"* and *"can play tricks on us."* Let's look at some examples.

The fragile porcelain child

Julio is ten years old. He was referred to me by a colleague who was unsure what was happening to him because he had displayed very worrying behaviors since he was a little boy. He is very rigid, prone to panic attacks, very anxious, and has had trouble sleeping at night since he was a baby. He is straightforward, lively, and expressive during the interview with me. He tells me that he gets things in his head that don't go away and that one day he saw a program on TV about brain chemistry and thinks he has a messed-up chemistry. Communicating with him is good; he pays close attention to what I ask and seems eager to stop suffering. He tells me that he has an older brother but that his brother is very lucky to be the oldest because their mother leaves him alone, but, being the youngest, he is not so fortunate, and that as long as he does not have a younger brother for the mother to deal with; he told me, verbatim, *"That's the way it is."*

He tells me that sometimes it is hard to breathe, that he feels like he is going to die, experiences an intense tightness in his chest, and that he *"feels terrible."* He is obviously describing the symptoms of an anxiety crisis or panic attack. His verbal skills for his age are excellent. He seems intelligent and is doing well in school and with friends. He tells me he has discovered that *"people like him"* sometimes wash their hands repeatedly, but it hasn't happened to him. What comes to

DOI: 10.4324/9781003581543-5

his mind repeatedly is that something bad will happen, but he doesn't know what or why. But those things don't leave his mind.

We arranged to meet another day, and I decided to talk to the parents. After beginning the talk with them, the mother immediately acknowledges that she is very controlling, and the father comments that sometimes it is impossible to *"bear it."* He tells her to leave *"the child"* alone, but that he has never been able to restrain the mother in her intense desire to control and that he's given her up as impossible. He is very respectful of his wife's difficulties, which is a very favorable indicator.

The mother, downcast and incredibly guilty, confirms this is how it is, but she cannot help it. I tell her it is courageous to acknowledge to me, a complete stranger, that these difficulties exist. I suggest they investigate what is happening so that I can help not only their child but them as well.

It seems that almost the whole family, except for the eldest, is involved in a vicious circle from which they have been unable to escape and, thus, need help. In this situation, I do not propose a parents' work group, but the best thing is a specific space for the mother to see what is happening to her and why. My impression is that she sees her son as very fragile, weak, and in danger, and, thanks to her exhaustive control, she is keeping him *"protected and safe."* In other words, there is a noticeable discrepancy between the boy's personality and the personality the mother attributed to him. The task was to discover why and help the mother differentiate her son from one she imagined.

The mother agreed to have several interviews to learn what was happening to her. Her willingness made things much smoother. We soon found out what was going on. The mother told me that she had a brother with a disease that caused him to fall all the time and that he always had one broken bone or another. Her mother died when she was young, and she became the mother of the house. All the responsibility fell on her, including making sure that nothing happened to her brother, which was difficult since he fell easily. The *"premature"* mother suffered a lot, felt very responsible, and tried to do well, but despite very exhaustive control, it was impossible to avoid injuries to her brother. I won't go any further, but I think the problem lay in the fact that the mother only felt she was a good mother to the extent that she could protect and achieve with her son the *"success"* she thought she did not have with her brother (*this is the mirror effect*), and thus alleviate the intense feelings of guilt she attributed to herself, undeservedly, in her role as a mother.

Little by little, things were resolved when she understood that she blamed herself for not achieving *"the impossible"* and that she did not value herself for having accomplished many things *"that it was possible to achieve,"* such as her son being honest, sincere, responsible, which clearly indicated her good work as a mother. It was also necessary for her son to receive therapeutic help.

The *"poor thing's syndrome"* and the pain of grief

Alberto is a 13-year-old teenager who was referred to me because he is starting to have serious problems with alcohol. During the weekends, he overdoes it and loses control; he does not exhibit violent behaviors in his lack of control; instead, he is defiant and contemptuous towards his friends and displays a striking arrogance that goes beyond what is expected in a teenager. Unable to pick up his room or do his homework, Alberto seems to be a boy who waits for things to fall into his lap rather than trying to get them. In other words, he contrasted excessive arrogance and exhibitionism with passivity at all levels. Of course, he flirted with girls little or not at all, although the first impression was that he was a flirt. At school, he seemed to have found a good place as the *"class clown,"* for which he received some recognition and respect from his classmates. However, his excesses made him lose friends quickly, at the same speed with which sand from the beach slips through your fingers.

His desperate parents did not know what to do. The father was a busy professional with little time to spend at home. The mother did not work and was very dedicated to the son's upbringing, which did not seem to bother her. During the interview, the mother was in charge of talking about the child, and the father said nothing. She was the one *"responsible,"* not him. Occasionally, she would say, *"I just don't have time,"* as if she was ashamed and blaming herself. This behavior conveyed that the authoritative voice was that of the mother.

I will not go into other details of the case regarding placing limits for adolescents and other issues, but I will explain what happened. In the work with the parents, we soon saw that the mother had experienced some traumatic situations that, in my opinion, were decisive. We had talked and seen how the mother did everything for the son with phrases that justified her action, such as *"poor thing, he must be tired,"; "poor thing, he has a cold"; "Poor thing . . . ."* I was struck by the fact that Alberto was a *"poor thing,"* according to the mother. But what made the mother insistently consider her son a *"poor thing"*? She was assigning him a personality that had little or nothing to do with him (*the mirror effect*). At one point, and in passing, I was told that the mother had suffered several miscarriages and that they had had a hard time having children. The mother and father, with tears in their eyes, told me about one of the miscarriages in particular, at a few weeks' gestation, a baby whom they were going to name Alberto. This was a very painful moment for them and me. The pain mixed with the devastating feeling of absolute desolation. How much these parents have suffered!

In my opinion, it was clear who the *"poor things"* were; they were the babies who did not make it to birth and whom both the mother and father felt they were not able to protect. When they had the first baby, the fear of losing him was so great that she needed to protect him, something she felt she had not done with the unborn babies. The father understood that it had to be this way and that he should not interfere with the protection that the mother provided. That is to say, the mother needed help to process the grief, to see that what she considered the best protection was overprotection. The father needed help to understand that his restraint was of little help and thus broke the vicious circle that had been established.

Whereas the mother was devastated, the father was also broken down and stuck. This made him act like a father who was afraid to intervene. I explained that somehow his son was looking for a parent to reach out to him to set boundaries and to be more present in his life, but that the broken state he was in had paralyzed him. So, in my view, it was not so much the mother's need for overprotection that was the central cause of the difficulties, but rather the absence, because of the breakdown, of the father and his functions. The son was somehow *"demanding"* an authority figure to intervene in the face of his out-of-control behavior. To me, it was a blatant appeal to the father. When I explained this to the parents, the mother was relieved to think that, as she told me, *"Not everything is the mother's responsibility."* I replied of course not. To help them further in their grieving, I told them that neither mothers nor fathers are responsible for what nature sometimes throws at us. They understood it at once. I thought that the father had become so blocked and bewildered that he had taken refuge in work to deal with his grief, which meant another type of grief for him: that of not being a father when nature did not interfere with the birth of his child. Over time, he grew closer to his son and fatherhood, including his maternal aspects.

I wanted to comment on these two situations so that we can see how, when it comes to defining the personality of our children, our own experiences also influence, condition, and intervene. This is not bad; it's just how it is. Another thing is that, in complex cases, reviewing as much information as possible is necessary, so it is convenient to work side by side with the parents. If we take a closer look, we will see how diagnoses can change as we get more information. In this case, if we had stopped at the child's behavior, the diagnosis would have been *"behavioral disorder with antisocial behavioral traits."* If we had focused on the mother's trauma, we would speak of a *"depressed mother and overprotective functioning with secondary tyrannizing of the child."* When arriving at the absence of the father's role, we could have diagnosed *"absent father syndrome."* Trying to understand everything that is happening is what will help us the most, along the lines of the phrase attributed to St. Thomas Aquinas: *"Beware the man of one book."*

In the second case, there was another crucial element for things to work out. The son did not need treatment. The father's increased involvement and effectiveness were sufficient. Why? In addition to their total willingness, the parents consulted me in time, allowing the son's behaviors not to settle in definitively. That is why I recommend not delaying and not falling into the trap of *"he will get over it."* The time lost can cause many of these behaviors, initially reactive, to become consolidated and, thus, dramatically worsen the prognosis and the chances of resolution.

When I refer to an increase in the father's effectiveness, I don't just mean that he should set limits for the son. I also mean he talked to him more, told him that he is not happy with so much defiance or that he gets too angry, and they did activities together, he spent time with him, etc. There is often the illusion that just setting limits is enough, but it is not.

On the other hand, the first psychoanalytic reference to a father helping his son through the psychoanalyst was Freud's famous *"little Hans"* case, in which Freud points out different aspects to the father and the latter in turn to his son, or, what I have come to call *"psychoanalysis for parents,"* which, for my part, I do not consider an *"originality"* or anything new. Let us remember that little Hans's fears prompted the father to consult Freud. In the next chapter, I will comment on the situations that constitute severe warnings from the children in search of help. For little Hans's father, it was the fear expressed by his son. Children's fears are one of the critical warning signs that something is wrong.

Reference list

Bion, W. (1959). Attacks on linking. *The International Journal of Psychoanalysis*, 40:308.

Britton, R. (1998). Subjectivity, objectivity, and potential space. In *Belief and imagination*. Routledge.

Britton, R. (2004). Subjectivity, objectivity, and triangular space. *The Psychoanalytic Quarterly*, 73:47–61.

Fonagy, P., and Target, M. (1996). Predictors of outcome in child psychoanalysis: A retrospective study of 763 cases at the Anna Freud Center. *Journal of the American Psychoanalytic Association*, 44:27–73.

Freud, S. (1922). *Análisis de la fobia de un niño de cinco años*. Obras Completas de Sigmund Freud, Vol. 10. Ed. Amorrortu.

García-Castrillón, C. (2007). *Ser padres, ¿una misión imposible?* Ed. Glosa.

Mannoni, M. (1974). *El Niño, su Enfermedad y los Otros*. Tel-Aviv: Am Oved.

Weisse, E. (1960). *The structure and dynamics of the human mind*. New York: Grune & Stratton.

Chapter 5

Recognizing red flags in children

Cayetano García-Castrillón Armengou

Sometimes, the symptom is given too much importance, and the con-flicting origin of the symptom is neglected. In fact, there is a tendency to turn symptoms into illnesses. It would seem that *"the patient hinders the clinical, the symptomatology does not."* It is not that symptoms are not significant; they are *"also"* important, but we cannot disregard the person and their circumstances. We run the risk of talking too much about symptoms and illnesses and not enough about families and their difficulties. This deviation can lead to an intense approach to treating the symptom but no attention to the origin of the conflict that may be generating it. Four possible risks result from doing so:

1. The medicalization of the child and adolescent population.
2. The exclusion of parents as essential help.
3. The *"chronification"* of mental pathology in childhood and adolescence.
4. The denial that conflicts exist.

While symptoms are often easily detected by their evidence, it is more difficult to detect and obtain information about the underlying con-flicts. We could say that this information is less in plain sight. Hence, the importance of knowing that children and adolescents give us infor-mation about themselves in several ways:

1. What they do or do not tell us.
2. Their way of playing and the games they play.
3. The drawings they make or what they create.
4. Their demeanor, behavior, and reactions.
5. Their way of interacting with others.

DOI: 10.4324/9781003581543-6

If a child or adolescent is having a hard time, they will express the problem in one of these ways. Obviously, what parents tell us is crucial for my colleagues and me. Not only the data on the child's progress but also their opinions, worries, fears, ways of interacting, ways of managing conflicts, ways of handling authority, emotional reactions that the children provoke, academic experiences, and so on. No less important is the information that teachers can provide us with. As you will observe, the more we know, the better.

Let's look at some brief examples of what parents told me before I saw their children and their drawings.

- Parents: *"My son is incredibly reserved and inhibited and plays little at school"* (9 years old, draws swimming pool, people without arms; Figure 5.1).
- Parents: *"My child is very attention-seeking"* (4 years old, drawing of a propped-up heart; Figure 5.2).
- Parents: *"My daughter dresses up in costumes often"* (7 years old, draws empty head; Figure 5.3).

Figure 5.1 "*Quiet boy*" makes this drawing.

Figure 5.2 The "attention seeker" draws this one. What is it? A heart that does not support itself.

Figure 5.3 This is the one of the girl who dresses up.

Figure 5.4 The 10-year-old boy draws this picture.

- Parents: *"My son is chubby. He's 10 years old, and we don't think he's handling it well"* (draw fight; Figure 5.4).

These parents detected the symptoms and were alarmed. Instead of dismissing their concerns, they were able to consider that something was wrong and consult with someone. These are the drawings:

If we pay attention, we already have two sources of information: what the parents mentioned and the drawings (I like to say that drawings are the best projective tests for children. Incidentally, I am not the only one who says so).

If we put together the information from the parents and the drawing, we can already formulate some hypotheses. I won't go into too much detail. These were my initial ideas.

First case: The boy told me that the people in the pool were his family, and I was struck by the fact that they had no arms. It could be possible that the boy was quiet because he lacked hugs, acceptance, and family support, and that was inhibiting him. Obviously, I shared this hypothesis with his parents.

Second case: The parents told me that he sought attention and that the drawing was a heart, which, as the child told me, would not fall. In short, a propped-up heart. It would be possible then that attention-seeking was, for this boy, a way of ensuring he was loved.

Third case: The girl who dresses up in costumes and draws a picture with an empty head. She may not dare to be herself.

Fourth case: The *"chubby"* boy (according to the parents) draws a fight, someone who bothers another person, a conflicting situation. Is it at school or at home where the clash is? Would the *"chubby thing"* be the expression of an excess of anxiety calmed down with food? When I asked him about it, he told me that it was because of his fights with his mother.

All this information gathering will compel us to form a hypothesis about what could be happening, which is our objective, first and foremost.

Why hypotheses matter in understanding behavior

It does not matter if the hypothesis is wrong; hypotheses may be expanded, discarded, and modified as we learn more about each case. To do this, we will check whether the hypothesis is true or not. How do we do this check? Well, by asking. In the first case, we could ask, for example: *"Do you want to be with your parents more?"* In the second case, I would ask if he thought that if his parents are not paying attention to him constantly, it is because they do not love him. In the third situation, I would ask, for example, if she is afraid to say what she thinks; and in the fourth case, I would be direct, asking what happens with Mom, or what do you think is wrong with your mom (which is what I asked him). Little by little, you will be able to find out where the origin of the conflict is as the *"analysis"* and *"investigation"* progresses.

I have focused on this aspect to convey how important it is to ask questions and that parents should also be encouraged to do so and not demand to know everything from the outset. This greatly enhances the dialogue. Although this is my consulting office, I believe that parents can also try to make their hypotheses by gathering information. They can also ask questions. Possibly, many *"ambiguities"* will be dispelled without having to seek professional help. After all, dealing with conflicts is also part of a parent's day-to-day life. However, the tendency to focus exclusively on behavior (or *"bad"* behavior) closes off the possibility of also probing at home. This is not the parents' fault. In times of stress, the ability to reflect, stop, and restrain oneself is much more difficult. Parents need to be aware of this highly reactive emotional phenomenon because they can avoid being blocked as long as they are aware of it.

To expect all parents to be patient, understanding, and open to dialogue at all times is a magnificent fantasy, but it is far from reality. Moreover, as I will explain later, the parents' correction in how they deal with situations will serve as a clear example to their children. They will also be able to change thanks to the example of their parents.

That is to say, thanks to the hypotheses, we will know what to ask and thus take stock. A hypothesis is better, even if false, than putting a *"label"* on the child. It will be quite harmful because we will leave the factors causing the problems out of our *"inquiry and investigation."* Thus, in the best case, we will not help at all, and in the worst case, we will become involuntary collaborators in the *"chronification of the conflict."* In addition, the label often has an accusatory character. Frequent phrases, such as the following, indicate this: *"he just doesn't feel like talking," "he just wants attention," "she plays dress-up,"* etc. For me, an already labeled child or adolescent poses an alarming situation.

Warning signs that call for attention

We must also consider the warning signs, which represent a risk in themselves. It would be worrying if they are overlooked by parents, pediatricians, teachers, or anyone else. We have the following:

1. **The slowing down of the child's development**
   The slowing down of the child's development, going more slowly, falling behind the class, not connecting, not adjusting more or less to the demands, etc. Although they do not usually consult because of a specific symptom, they do so because they are concerned about the child's progress in general.

   Here's an example: Pepe, a 7-year-old boy who doesn't know what to put in his planner. He is completing his last assignments, gets stuck, is distracted, and doesn't finish. The teacher is concerned, and the parents are as well. The parents start demanding that he tell them what is wrong, and he says he doesn't know. The parents get angry and punish him, and the teacher tells them that he may have to repeat if he continues like this. The parents become even more alarmed, thinking that if he is so young and already going to repeat, *"not good."* This leads to more demands, pressures, and endless tensions, which reach a *crescendo* as the days go by without any change for the better, but rather for the worse.

Driven by desperation, in a last attempt to fix what they feel is a dramatic future for their son, the father becomes strict, and the mother becomes controlling. The mother, trying to control the academics, contacts other mothers at the school through WhatsApp to get information about the homework her son has been assigned and that he, mentally blocked, has forgotten. This has been going on for a year and a half. Understandably, with that tension, little progress can be made. When I asked the parents more about the boy outside of academics, they told me that he is afraid to play soccer with other children, doesn't seem interested, and is very protective of his little brother. Of course, they were already thinking he had a low IQ, ADHD, etc.

These *"hurricanes of anxiety"* are by themselves a symptom of alarm because we already know how things end up after a hurricane. In this case, what happened is that one day, the mother saw a strange drawing in the closet, full of scribbles of many dark colors, and asked the boy what it was. The answer was blunt: *"That's me, a piece of junk."* The mother raised the alarm, saying, *"My son is depressed."* She was right, and the father also understood it that way. These parents gathered the information and formed a correct hypothesis that allowed them to seek help. From then on, by treating the depression with therapy and some parental guidance, everything changed. As always, little by little.

The son's answer lingered with the mother, and she did not discard that information; she wondered why her son saw himself as a *"piece of shit"* and thought that this must be very painful for him. I told them that, of course, it was not at all pleasant for the boy; if he already felt like *"crap,"* he would feel worse every time criticism and failures came, and that the risk was that he would end up believing that he really was a hopeless disaster. That is why these hurricanes of anxiety are so harmful because they destroy any hope of change, improvement, self-esteem, etc.

This impeccably attentive listening by the mother, and later by the father, allowed for emotional contact that was getting blocked with homework, failures, punishments, demands, etc. I told the parents that with such a low, negative, and pessimistic concept they had of their son, he could have little hope and expectations of himself. After all, as I told them, *"You can't get much out of a piece of crap. The only thing you can expect from a piece of crap is to get it out of the way."* In other words, he must have had such a devalued concept of himself that he was sinking, and how much he must have suffered if he understood that others were lucky enough not to be a *"piece of crap like him."* That's why he didn't play soccer. Later, when talking to the boy, it became clear that he was at rock bottom and a clear risk of suicide and that all the coercive measures being taken only aggravated the situation. These parents' understanding and their sensitivity helped their son enormously. The school was alerted that he was depressed, and the teacher cooperated by giving him more leeway. The father adopted a closer relationship with his son, talking and playing more with him, and the mother became less controlling. Everyone flourished. That said, we worked at it for quite some time.

2. **Repeated attention-seeking behavior**

Repeated attention-seeking behavior, whatever the nature. It is essential to know that children, unlike adults, usually lack words and verbal expressiveness to describe their feelings and emotional states, and what they do is express them through their behavior. What does it mean to *"express them"* with their behavior?

Let's look at an example. I should clarify that, often, part of my professional task is to seek the help and support of the teachers who are with the children daily. They have always collaborated, which is something to be grateful for.

One teacher told me, *"I have a 6-year-old boy who goes out, comes in, gets up, approaches me affectionately, interrupts me constantly." Because* of this, the teacher felt sorry for the boy, who didn't even get angry with her when she punished him or called him to order. This caught her attention. She brought me a series of drawings. All of them showed blood: mouth, arm, and on the belly. The teacher would ask him what it was, and he would say *"blood,"* so she didn't know if what he wanted was to get attention, and that was it. I told her that it seemed to me that, indeed, he did want to draw attention to himself, but that, unfortunately, this way of children drawing attention is attributed a pejorative meaning that provokes a rejection of them, but that he probably wanted to draw attention to himself because he was trying to convey that something was wrong with him and that he did not know what to do.

The child, who is six years old, cannot say, *"Look, sir, this painful situation is happening at home."* No child can express himself like that, and they resort to calling attention in their own way. Therefore, we must know where we have to pay attention. In this boy, it was clearly the blood. We must be careful not to fall into the serious mistake of accusing the child of manipulation because if we do so, far from attending to the child, we push him away and condemn him. And when a child has anxiety, he does not stop; he warns, complains, and calls for attention because he cannot contain himself and looks for the adults to contain him. When faced with a problem, children cannot stop by themselves. Finally, what happened was that he watched a lot of violent movies with little or no supervision from his parents, who were distracted.

3. *"Glued"* **children**

Children who are *"glued"* to their parents. I am referring to children who are superglued to their parents.

The following would be a clear example. The parents of Javier, who is eight years old, consult me because he gets into bed with them, is afraid at night, does not let his brother touch his toys, and plays war constantly. He prepares the battlefield meticulously with strategically placed soldiers. According to what the father tells me, he is a real *"military strategist."* I wondered what the boy's enemies could be. As I mentioned before, not only are the pictures important, but also what and how children play. The parents get angry but are reluctant to do so because they say he is a good boy, studies, behaves well, and does what he is asked for at home, although he is jealous of his brother and gets truly angry when his brother takes his toys. His parents tell me that they tell him he is older and that since his brother is *"little,"* he has to share his toys with him. I told them both, no. I said that the little one must learn that what is not his is not his. They could unintentionally make him believe that his brother has to give him everything because he is the youngest and that their eldest son feared that war would break out when he could no longer cope with the situation. They commented that the boy even *"strategically"* hid his favorite toys so his brother would not see them. Logically, I believe that the boy also thought he would not only be left without toys but also, due to his anger, without parents, so he clung to them to calm his fears.

4. **ADHD diagnoses**

ADHD diagnoses are alarming because of the high percentage of false positives. This implies revising the diagnoses, or at least that is what I do. In my opinion, systematically turning a symptom into a disease, attention deficit and hyperactivity, has generated many false diagnoses. In the face of any conflict, attention is always diminished; that is the most typical reaction. As I explained before, children express themselves a lot with their behavior. A nervous child is rarely still. It also happens to us adults, although ours is usually more of a mental hyperactivity. On the contrary, the diagnosis of ADHD can also be overlooked due to the lack of frequent or recurring symptoms. Therefore, in any case, each situation should be thoroughly reviewed. Remember that the best treatment is the best diagnosis.

A brief example. Rodrigo, 11 years old, is distracted, restless, underachiever, etc. The parents told me, *"We already know what he has; they told us he has ADHD."* Meanwhile, I was thinking I had no idea where things were going. Besides, they couldn't be entirely convinced if they came to ask me. When I talked to Rodrigo, he was very anxious and jumpy. I told him I wouldn't understand anything if he spoke so fast. He took a breath and told me: *"My grandmother and my grandfather died almost at the same time; I don't know why that happened. I just feel like crying in class, and I'm afraid they'll tell me I'm mental if they notice that sometimes I cry. I put my hands up, and they don't notice."* I didn't need to ask him what was wrong. Nonetheless, if we had focused on *"only"* the symptoms, the diagnosis of ADHD would have been apparent, but the possibility of approaching the emotional world would have been blocked. This bright boy was able to express the reason for his suffering clearly. I think that sometimes, we adults are the ones who get *"hung up"* because we can also be overexcited by anxiety, but we can *"get off the hook"* with a little deliberation.

5. **Nonspecific tummy aches**

Nonspecific tummy aches, the body as the scene of the conflict: It happened to little Martita, seven years old, who only had tummy aches from Sunday to Thursday, just before school. On Fridays, she didn't have them. The little girl found it hard to leave her mother's side to attend school.

6. **Academic failure**

   Countless studies indicate that 80% of academic failure is attributable to emotional problems.

7. **Any suicidal ideation**

   Any suicidal ideation at any age should be treated with the utmost interest and rigor. Never trivialize these thoughts under any circumstances, and seek immediate professional help.

8. **The sudden appearance of hostile behavior**

   The sudden appearance of hostile behavior and confrontations, which are entirely out of the ordinary, with parents or siblings may express the existence of bullying. Bullied children suffer so much and put up with so much that they tend to *"explode"* uncontrollably at home. If, along with this, there is a sudden drop in academic performance, loss of desire to go to school, fear of going, and sadness, this problem is highly likely occurring. Collaboration and a good partnership with teachers will, as always, help a lot.

   Albert is an 11-year-old boy—pleasant, cheerful—who one day told his mother that he was not going to school anymore. There was no way he was going. This angered the mother, who did not understand why. When she asked her son why he wasn't going, Albert said he couldn't tell her. The mother noticed that when he answered that he could not tell her, he became incredibly nervous.

   One day, the school called to tell her that there had been an accident, that her son had been taken to the hospital, that it was not serious, and that she should come. Albert's arm was broken. In tears and despair, he confessed to his mother that some older boys were beating him up, and this time, they threw him down the stairs. The mother asked him why he had not told her before. He answered, *"If I told you, it would be worse; if the older children found out, they would beat me even more. That's what they told me."* As we can see, the situation was terrible. Albert was terrified. This traumatic impact explained his sudden mood swings, the tantrums at home, and his panic over going to school. But he also panicked about going outside, and even in the supermarket, he constantly looked out for *"the older kids."* Albert's recovery was long and difficult. In addition, he had to change schools.

9. **The lies**

   When the child sometimes does not tell the whole truth, they hide it. A little lie from a child does not have the depth of an adult's lie. Many times, it is a way to preserve their intimacy or, and this is the most common, to calm their fear of being scolded. This is important to keep in mind so as not to treat it in the same way as an adult lie, with saying things like, *"I don't trust you anymore,"* *"You don't keep your word,"* *"You should be ashamed of yourself,"* etc.

It's better to ask, *"Why were you afraid to tell me what really happened? Did you think we were going to be very angry with you?"* or say something like, *"By lying, you add the problem that it will be harder for us to believe or trust you, and that's a shame."* Typically, children say they are afraid of being scolded, and this fear of scolding is even more intense in adolescents. In short, if we were to assign the same adult meaning to the child, we would be setting up a very distorted scenario for our child, making us very defensive and angry. If we manage to de-dramatize these minor day-to-day conflicts, so much the better.

But if we observe the continuous use of lies or even if the stories associated with the lie begin to be believed by the child, then we will be facing a serious problem. Obviously, this behavior seriously damages the parents' confidence in their children. Constant victimization is an expression of lying. Both are serious and require immediate intervention. In addition, one of the problems associated with lying or victimization is that they generate a feeling of domination, triumph, and superiority over others, which— de facto—are emotionally addictive. That is, a kind of enjoyment of control and manipulation over others is associated with a sense of impunity, an absence of risk and danger. This explains the need to promptly intervene so that the enticement generated by *"dominance"* is not solidified. As we can see, it is not only drugs or devices that create addictions but also certain experiences.

10. **Prevention of sexual abuse**

In the prevention of sexual abuse in childhood, it is very important to warn children that no one should *"touch"* them and that if it happens, they should not be afraid to say it. Often, a symptom that something may happen is that they do not want to go with certain people, that they insist on not going, that they are suddenly sad, closed in on themselves, and scared.

Other symptoms

- The lack of non-verbal communication, an inexpressive baby leaves an impact by creating the feeling of emptiness when observing it, that it does not interact with the mother or the environment, falls within the autistic range.

- That he doesn't play, is always in his own world, and shows apathy.
- In early ages, the appearance of obsessive rituals requires immediate intervention, as they solidify quickly. This is an emergency.
- Need for immediate satisfaction and enormous intolerance to frustration, with the progression of increasing tantrums.
- Children who have an excessive desire to dominate and impose their rules on others. If they lose, they always change the rules to their benefit.
- When parents say that the child is good, perfect. Well, that's not a child. He represses all the friction of development. This hyper-good or hyper-invisible syndrome gives food for thought.
- Children who have lost their *"curiosity."*
- It is worrying that adults consider *"nonsense"* to be what children tell them.
- The denial of the presence of difficulties in the family.
- An excess of pride in the parents that blinds them, and they dig in their heels.
- Symptoms of severe pathologies: delirium, severe insomnia, etc.
- Addictions. One of the most frequent problems is the time they spend on the cell phone or gaming console skyrockets, usually at night, interfering with sleep and generating a sleep deficit.[1] In short, a striking excess of tiredness and fatigue throughout the day should be examined.
- The appearance of eating problems accompanied by an obsession with body image and an exacerbated perfectionist component.
- In addition to a constant impulsive performance.

These are some prominent symptoms to look out for. Obviously, these are not all of them, just the most significant. If you observe any of the preceding items, you can clarify the situation a lot by consulting a professional.

Note

1 As I will show later, awareness of the passage of time is altered by the use of devices (Chapter 12).

Reference list

Balint, M. (1968). *The basic fault*. London: Tavistock Publications.

Bion, W. R. (1959). Attacks on linking. *International Journal of Psychoanalysis*, 40:308–315.

Jacobs, L. (ed.) (2008). *Parent-centered child therapy: Attachment, identification, and reflective functions*. Lanham, MD: Jason Aronson.

Lingiardi, V., and McWilliams, N. (2017). *Psychodynamic diagnostic manual*, 2nd Edition. Guilford.

Meltzer, D. (1975). Adhesive identification. *Contemporary Psychoanalysis*, 11:289.

Torras, E. (2012). *Normalidad, psicopatología y tratamientos en niños, adolescentes y familia*. Barcelona: Ed. Octaedro.

Weisse, E. (1960). *The structure and dynamics of the human mind*. New York: Grune & Stratton.

Winnicott, D. (1953). Transitional objects and transitional phenomena-A study of the first not-me possession. *The International Journal of Psychoanalysis*, 34:89.

Part II

Growing as parents, thriving as a family

Chapter 6

Divine parents or human parents?

Cayetano García-Castrillón Armengou

Parents are human, not divine, which is, in principle, an advantage. Although we would all like to be divine, we are not. Let's imagine a tennis player who would like to be divine and therefore demands it of himself. For example, Rafael Nadal would expect not to miss any balls and win all the games, sets, and matches, and with that, he would claim to be good, that is to say, that only this way would he believe that he is good. There would come a moment in which he would feel enormous stress, not only when entering the court but also when missing a ball or losing a game or a set, since he could experience a feeling of enormous personal failure because, deep down and without detecting it, he was demanding himself to be divine and perfect.

At a given moment, if this internal pressure were to press him too hard and he could no longer bear such a negative idea of himself, Nadal would possibly start to say, *"I am not the disaster; I am divine, and what sucks is the racquet, or the court, or the balls, or the specta-tors."* He would start to unload this unbearable internal reproach by turning it outwards, probably with great certainty that the problem is outside and not in him (externalization). The other option would be a massive internalization (in the form of constant self-criticism) with serious risks of entering a tailspin into depression. Since he does not consider himself divine, fortunately for Nadal and us, if he fails, he will try to recover or improve in the next ball, set, or tournament (as he has shown us).

I give this example because, whether as parents or in any facet of our lives, we would love to be divine, but we are not! If we are not aware of this and, as a consequence, we are excessively hurt or frus-trated by our inevitable failures or lapses, we will feel pressured to want to do everything right at *"all times and at any cost."* It is possible

DOI: 10.4324/9781003581543-8

then that what would happen to Nadal, who was trapped by the desire to be divine, could happen to us and that we also begin to externalize. But being parents, on whom are we going to externalize? Well, on our children. So, the divine Nadal would do it to the court, the racket, etc., and we will do it to our children so that we will feel that our (childish) fantasy of divinity remains intact as long as we externalize (like the tennis player who breaks the racket). Sometimes, the externalization of parents falls on the school teachers to include their child in the divine group, with the illusory pretension of freeing us from guilt, from the feeling of failure, from impotence, thus preserving our self-esteem, etc. However, with children, the same as in a tennis match, you know how you start, but you do not know how everything is going to go due to two fundamental reasons:

1. Children go through different stages during their development; there are times when there are significant changes, and each child also has their own personality.
2. In parallel, we, the parents, will encounter these changes. In addition, we have our concerns, moments, personal histories, and personalities.

In this sense, from the moment our baby is born, or even before, we imagine what they will be like. We will be subjected to a constant process of adaptation, in which a child can significantly activate mom and dad's feelings: on many occasions, our state of mind is subject to and will depend on the progress, evolution, or involution of our children; therefore, we are very dependent on them.

In other words, with changes in their evolution, or if there is a problem, we must also deal with *"how we feel or how they make us feel."* Sometimes, these feelings can be challenging to deal with. For example, a child who is sad and not getting good grades will leave us worried because he is not doing well, and his future will arouse intense concern. This can make us so uncomfortable that we want to resolve it quickly, so we will need the child to fix it as rapidly if the activated feeling is complex and difficult to tolerate. I call this haste *"the acceleration spiral."* We may become very insistent: *"Son, pass once and for all. This uneasiness is hard for me, and only you can prevent it"*—without detecting that there may be an underlying sadness, for example, which is usually the most frequent factor. Children become depressed, anxious, fearful, insecure, etc.

When this happens, the way we adapt or manage the situation is marked by haste, not realizing that our main objective is to get rid of the stress as quickly as possible. This makes it difficult for us to think about what might be happening to our son or daughter. In other words, impulse takes over. This is very common hastiness because it is human to want to eliminate the problem as soon as possible since it causes us suffering and pain. But, as the saying goes, *"haste makes waste."*

Knowing about this haste, or possible haste, can help us avoid falling into the trap because it is a relatively automatic reaction. One day, a father told me: *"This child of mine is worse than a toothache."* If we are in a hurry to relieve ourselves of toothaches, it will not be less so with our children. It is crucial to be attentive to this spontaneous reaction.

Typically, when attending to parents, my first objective is to contain this haste and promote dialogue, creativity, and a better relationship with the children. Meanwhile, the parents want the child to study, behave well, etc., once and for all, or *"for once and for all, damn it."* With hastiness, many aspects collapse, including dialogue and the ability to think.

If haste is already established, which, as I mentioned, is a common reaction, the tendency to increase the need to *"control"* rises because, hypothetically, everything will be solved sooner if our son or daughter does everything we tell him or her to do. *"We have tried everything,"* and this way, we are very much on top of them, but without dialogue.

In addition, during a child's development, there are phases where new aspects appear, and novelties can worry us. If we look at each change in our children's development, there is a common denominator if things are going well: the child gains a little more autonomy. For example, he stops breastfeeding and starts to take a bottle, and then he wants to pick it up; he begins to crawl or walk, so he starts to move away from us. We experience some of these changes towards greater autonomy with joy: the child is walking, talking, picking up the bottle by himself, etc., because we realize this has to do with progress. But sometimes, for example, concerning feeding, he displays this greater autonomy by saying that he does not want more, does not like something, or does not eat everything we put in front of him. We do not see it as an advancement of our child but as the fact that we cannot control everything anymore, that not everything is in our hands, and we get scared. The feeling is activated in us, and, at the same time, the fear that things *"can get out of hand."*

Another typical situation is when he is already walking and moves away from us, and we tell him to come, and he does not; if we try to put him in the stroller, he refuses, arches his back, wants to be taken by the hand or held in our arms. In other words, he moves away, wanting to make his own decisions *"little by little"* as he grows. This process of autonomy and separation that evolves gradually will inevitably mean a different experience for each of us.

One of the most critical milestones happens around the age of three. They learn that *"no"* exists, but it is a *"no"* from a 3-year-old child, not the one we have in mind as adults. That is, it is a *"no"* to prove that they have some autonomy and something to say, almost a game. Later, in adolescence, it is reproduced with more intensity. This time, not only do we no longer control everything, but we are also faced with a *"no"* that sometimes leaves us feeling that we have no say over the situation. (A classic scenario is a girl who already wants to decide what clothes to wear and systematically refuses to wear what her mother tells her to wear).

That *"no,"* as I said, is almost like a game. However, if we understand it or translate it as an adult *"no"*—of the same caliber as the one we say to the phone salesman when he calls us at dinnertime to sell us anything—we will not differentiate it from the childish *"no"* or the adolescent *"no."* This will make us believe and interpret that the child no longer wants to have anything to do with us, that he defies our authority, wants to impose his holy will on us, rejects us, does not value us, and that he does not love us. We may react immediately by increasing control over him to the extent that we finally believe we are being defied. Not to mention, in adolescence, when they lock themselves in their room—that they never clean up—or conform to the rest of the traditional adolescent behaviors to emphasize their independence, such as being on their cell phone constantly, not coming home on time, telling us we know nothing about life or not telling us anything at all, at least directly, as they did when they were little. The reason is their intense need to preserve their privacy, indicating that they are no longer children and thus feel like adults. Let's remember that children hardly have any privacy.

Well, to a greater or lesser degree, throughout the development of our children, each advancement is, in the end, an aspect in which we do not *"apparently"* play much of a role. But we will be able to help them to enhance it if we don't panic too much. Then, we will be happy to see them share their achievements with us. In this way, we will play a significant role in their development.

Common parenting challenges

1. Action-reaction

Let's take, for example, a timid boy who does not get going, who does not want anyone to approach him, or the adolescent who, in the same way, is maintaining a blatant distance, and we notice, in both cases, that it is very difficult to get near them. Usually, when they start to open up—which is a big step in both cases—the shy kid will not normally do it by saying, *"Look, I have an emotional problem that prevents me from opening up,"* nor will the teenager say, *"I am overwhelmed because I don't know if I have friends or not, and that has prevented me from communicating better with you because I have realized that I take my stress out on you, and I want to put an end to that."* Obviously, they're not going to start opening up that way, but if anyone is willing to open up, it's a teenager.

They snap unexpectedly. They say, *"Leave me alone,"* etc. In other words, in their first contact—on their first serve, to continue the tennis analogy—they involuntarily provoke a reaction of discomfort in us, and, curiously, we are now the ones who do not feel like talking to them; we want to keep them away. They try to open up a little, but as they are afraid to open up at all, they prompt this reaction in us. It is very typical. I think it is imperative not to go into Newton's third law of action-reaction because it never works with children. They act in this way because it allows them to keep control of the situation, controlling the issue that *"really"* distresses them.

Parents are not the only ones who want to keep control; children do, too. It is a defense against anxiety in which it is convenient for us to keep us waiting, *"You are so angry, aren't you?"; "I didn't know I was such a bad parent,"* etc. If we *"take the bait"* and focus on saying only, *"That's not the way to talk in this house,"* everything will remain the same. So, I think it pays to be mindful of this. In my experience, asking them a question back without waiting for an answer is very practical. This keeps a window open instead of *"slamming the door"* and shutting down communication.

Recently, a mother was telling me that she noticed that her daughter always came to argue with her when she was upset. She discovered this because one day, she asked her why she argued with her so much, and her daughter replied, *"Because I feel bad."* She then asked if it had always been like this, to which her daughter replied, *"Yes."* This is very common in children and adolescents, but it must be said that it is also common in adults.

2. **Rebelling**

On other occasions, we encounter a son or daughter's rebelliousness. Sooner or later, this rebelliousness will appear depending on their personality and moment of development, characteristically around age three and early adolescence. We tend to interpret rebelliousness as an outright rejection when what actually happens is that the child expresses their need to distance themselves, to have their privacy, to show their criteria, and to feel that they are someone who has a say.

But, since adolescents are often not very subtle when speaking out, we can interpret it as a strong challenge against us. If this happens, what follows is a sense of loss of control over our child, which causes us to become increasingly anxious, leading to a vicious rebellion-control circle. By jumping on them, the situation is strained repeatedly, which eventually leads to a *"very significant"* power struggle. What began with searching for one's own space, to differentiate oneself, and little else, can result in the previously-mentioned situation.

I think the best thing to do is to try not to get into this vicious circle. In my opinion, the most practical thing to do is, again, to ask the children the reason for their rebellion, *"Why are you acting like that?"* *"Did what I said bother you so much?"* With these types of questions, whether they answer us or not, we will move away from getting entangled in such a circle. This is not to say that it is easy to do it because a child, as I said before, stirs us a lot, but at least trying to do it can give us and give them a different option.

3. **Delayed contradictions**

Sometimes, we glaringly contradict ourselves, but not always in the moment. I call this *"delayed contradictions."* This is what often happens with cell phones or tablets. The cell phone has an enormous negative anxiolytic potential. So, as you may have noticed, it is not uncommon to see young children operating these devices or parents using them as pacifiers of the situation, for example, at mealtimes, to distract the child so everything runs smoothly. Similar scenarios are frequent when the parents resort to the cell phone to calm down, which transmits the idea that, in moments of great anxiety, worry, etc., the cell phone will be a *"relief."* Children learn this in such a way that, later on, when they find themselves in a situation that worries, distresses them, etc., they will follow our involuntary recommendation to turn to the cell phone. But now we will be more aware that, far from fixing one problem, it adds another.

We turn the cell phone into an instrument for relieving tension. That is why it is better to eat without a cell phone, to limit it, an awkward meal or encounter being preferable to anesthetizing it, thanks to the use and abuse of the cell phone.

4. **The cell phone *"as sedative"***

Let us look at three brief examples that show how the cell phone serves to relieve anxiety in the face of an underlying problem.

    a. A boy whose parents commented that he was glued to his cell phone all day and would not leave the house, that it was impossible for him to put it down despite punishments, cutting off his Wi-Fi, etc. The parents believed that all the problems started with using the cell phone. Digging into the son's background and talking to him, we discovered that he was painfully shy, had no confidence in making friends, and had thrown in the towel; he didn't even try. When he was little, his shyness was alleviated thanks to the efforts of his mother, who took him to his friends' various celebrations. This successful help from the mother allowed the problem not to grow, but it could not disappear completely. In adolescence, when he no longer went to any events, the problem flourished. This boy found in the cell phone the way out of his difficulties in relating to others, and as long as we did not understand these difficulties, we could hardly help him get rid of or detach from the cell phone. It was his only means of relief from his fear of not being able to have friends in other ways. It is very common that, while the cell phone decreases a son or daughter's anxiety, it simultaneously increases a parent's anxiety.

    b. A boy who did not stop playing a particular game on the tablet. Hours and hours. He mastered it to perfection. He knew all the tricks to win all the points and looked like a winner. The boy admitted that he even found it boring but spent hours playing the same game. Why was this happening even though the boy admitted that he was bored out of his mind?

After several inquiries, we concluded that the boy considered himself a failure, useless, that he would not achieve anything in life—very demanding of himself and very depressed—and that he needed to succeed at all costs with the game so as not to feel more depressed than he already felt. The game served as a way to offset those feelings but, at the same time, perpetuated the problem.

c. The girl in the photo. A 14-year-old girl continuously retouched her Instagram photos, obsessively, spending hours and hours of her day-to-day life, which meant a significant drop in her academic performance in a worrying way. We learned that she felt ugly, that this was unbearable to her, and that she feared that no boy would notice her if she didn't appear lustrous, beautiful, and retouched in front of others. Without these *"touch-ups,"* she feared that her social life would be seriously impaired and collapsed. From a preventive point of view, it is essential to warn our children that social media applications tend to show *"ideal"* people in all aspects, including physical ones, and that they should not believe everything they see. In short, all that glitters is not gold.

Cell phones, moreover, require so much time that they may even have skills that they do not develop due to lack of time. Let's remember the importance of boredom as an activator of creativity. I believe that we parents should not feel guilty if our children are bored. Boredom stimulates creativity and ingenuity.

These brief examples are the condensation of several weeks of work. It is not easy to understand the background of the problems right away. Presenting these brief examples may give rise to the idea that understanding is a quick process, but it never is. It requires thinking, testing, talking, raising hypotheses, discarding those we prove to be untrue, and looking for others, a work of mental research.

On the other hand, other sources of action-reaction influence our children. In particular, I will add what we could call externalization, which I have already mentioned before, meaning action-reaction-externalization. Let us now take a closer look at what this is all about.

Reference list

Balint, M. (1968). *The basic fault*. London: Tavistock Publications.

Freud, S. (1920). *Más allá del principio del placer*. Obras Completas de Sigmund Freud, Vol. 18. Ed. Amorrortu.

Meltzer, D. (1975). Adhesive identification. *Contemporary Psychoanalysis*, 11:289.

Steiner, J. (1997). *Refugios Psíquicos*. Biblioteca Nueva.

Torras, E. (2012). *Normalidad, psicopatología y tratamientos en niños, adolescentes y familias*. Barcelona: Ed. Octaedro.

Chapter 7

Action, reaction, and externalization

Understanding behavior

Cayetano García-Castrillón Armengou
and Blanca García-Castrillón Fernández

The profile

Let's imagine a mother who is a painter and is happy to be one. She learned to paint and is not frustrated because she's fulfilled her desire to paint. She has a daughter, for example, who is starting out, and the mother sees that she is not doing well, smudges too much, etc. If the mother has satisfied her desire, as I said before, observing her daughter's first steps in painting, she will likely understand that her daughter is in the process of learning, will not become demanding, and will be able to de-dramatize her mistakes. But if, for whatever reason, the mother did not fulfill the desire to become a painter, it may be that her frustration must be resolved through the daughter, pushing her with demands since she needs the daughter to resolve her frustration: *"You have to achieve what I could not."* In other words, *"You have to be the painter I could not be."* That is an externalization (projection).

It could also happen that, even having managed to become a painter and not become frustrated, the mother considers that, in this life, it is essential to be a painter. She believes it is a *"perfect profile"* that her daughter must fit, no matter what. Thus, she may have created a prototype of a divine daughter through which she understands that if her daughter fulfills it, everything will work out for her. This blocks the prevailing and correct idea that we are all different, including the parents and their children. In my observation, it is a common occurrence. When this happens, parents do not usually do it to impose their will but because they are frankly convinced that what has made them feel happy and satisfied in their lives will also make their children happy and satisfied.

DOI: 10.4324/9781003581543-9

However, if parents place all their peace of mind in their sons and daughters meeting that *"perfect profile"* when they demonstrate their own personality, tastes, and identities, which will necessarily be different from those of their parents, the latter may become very frightened and, in an attempt to calm their anxieties about the difference, start to exert enormous pressure to get their children to fit that profile. Or a child may be afraid to think about what they want to do in life. Sympathetically, I call it *"LinkedIn kids,"* where parents repeatedly check whether there is a match with the idealized profile. As soon as parents reflect on this idea, they will realize their misunderstanding.

Obviously, we all have a profile of how we would like our children to be, and sometimes we suffer frustrations. However, this is not a problem. The problem appears when a demanding process of externalization begins, which usually occurs when we are too scared by the things that distinguish us from our children. When, in reality, a son or daughter shows his or her styles, criteria, and tastes, it is because his or her parents, in one way or another, have conveyed to him or her enough *"confidence"* to do so. Something very positive that, often, the parents themselves do not value *"as their parental achievements."*

On the other hand, we must remember that our *"forgetfulness"* also contributes. I recently talked to a teacher[1] about a somewhat complicated adolescent student. She told me that the boy had had a confrontation with another teacher and that the teacher got angry and punished him by taking away his soccer ball. She told me that she spoke to the boy to ask him if it had been worth such a harsh confrontation with the teacher since, in her opinion, all he had gotten was the ball away from him. She said that the boy looked thoughtful. She then suggested he apologize to the teacher, as she thought he could get the ball back and have a better relationship with him. The boy apologized in the end. I told her that, in my opinion, she was an extraordinary teacher if it was of any use to her.

She thanked me and said, *"He's a teenager, and, of course, I'm young, and I remember when I also had those confrontations. I think I am more empathetic because of my age."* I replied that no, I thought she was more empathic because she *"hadn't forgotten"* her adolescence, and she replied, *"It's true. It was really just something typical of adolescents."* I told her that in psychoanalysis, that is called *"showing the path for repair"* because kids often get into trouble that they don't know how to get out of, and she showed her student a way out that he didn't know how to find.

We may wonder why the boy followed his teacher's advice. I think it was because she ultimately made him see that his action-reaction response cost him the ball. She would have acted like the boy if she had merely punished or scolded him. Because she remembered her adolescence, she didn't get caught up and helped him think through what his action-reaction didn't allow him to see.

Let's look at another example: Frank, 13 years old, repeatedly talks back to his father. The father considered this intolerable and took away his cell phone and other things. In other words, everything. At the same time, he told me that it hurt him to have taken all that away from his son and that he would not have done it if it were up to him. He asked me what to do in such cases, and he said he didn't know how to make his son see that talking to him that way was inappropriate. This is a typical example of adolescent action-reaction.

When I asked the father why he was uncomfortable with his decision, he said he knew it would not change anything. I agreed and told him that I thought it was very positive that he doubted the effectiveness of the measure, which would allow us to think about other less painful and, perhaps, more practical options, and that by reviewing what we're doing, we are taking a big step. Not only that, but the father's intuition also has more background; knowing that nothing would change was a clear approximation that the problem was not in the bad responses nor the use of the cell phone, Wi-Fi, or Netflix. In other words, it is like the doctor who realizes he has prescribed something for a different disease than the patient.

Finding out what was wrong with his son that caused him to react that way became a goal. That meant giving up the belief that *"taking more things away"* was worthwhile. After several meetings with the parents and the boy, I found that the three agreed when explaining the unrest. The boy had moved from a familiar middle school in a small town, where everyone knew each other, to a mega high school in the city, where the teachers were not as attentive to the students, nor did they all know each other as was the case at the other school. In addition, he did not fit in at first because the groups of kids were very closed off, and he did not know how to get along in *"that unfamiliar crowd."*

Frank was *"lost in the jungle,"* without many friends, and alone academically, and the impact was that his first grades were a disaster, even though Frank is an intelligent and brilliant student. This sunk him completely, and he answered rudely whenever he came home from school if his parents asked him about his studies. They were not used to it; they never thought their son would have academic problems. This made all the alarms *"go off,"* and they started to do an exhaustive follow-up of exams, homework, etc. All in all, everything became very tense. Both parents and children were so anxious and afraid that they got caught in an action-reaction relationship. This situation is frequent when children move from junior high to high school. Everyone undergoes a process of adaptation that can go well or not so well.

Breaking the cycle: Embracing imperfection in parenting

In short, I think it is imperative that we understand that neither we nor our children are ideal. They can provoke us a lot and send us into action-reaction relationship mode, which, if established, will lead us to rush and try to exercise intensive control over our children. They, in turn, will react by creating distance and seeking their space (curiously enough, this is their way of controlling their parents). Everyone, in the end, is trying to control the other. Obviously, this generates permanent familial tension since this configuration in the relationships is repeated like a loop, over and over again. On the other hand, if we are aware of this risk, remembering our childhood and adolescence, we will try not to create a profile for our children, to be careful not to make them the ones in charge of calming our frustrations, or not to turn them into the representation of our narcissistic anxieties. We must understand that they are different from us, that they can have problems and bad moments, and that if they mess up, it is not an absolute failure on our part as parents or theirs, etc., so it will be easier for us to be a little more patient and not go into action-reaction mode.

Another of the most severe risks that can emerge in the action-reaction mode is that we fall into a position of arrogance towards our children in which all the responsibility falls on them as the cause of all the problems. Sometimes, pride is associated with a powerful externalization towards children since it calms us down by making us feel and believe we do not make any mistakes. From then on, the responsibility will fall totally on them: they do not study, talk back, spend too much time on their cell phone, etc. Let's remember that, in general, acknowledging our mistakes or limitations is not appetizing for anyone.

Pride can make us think that the best way to help our children is to correct them continually. This, in turn, leads to a hidden *"declaration of war"* and significant and reciprocal resentment between parents and children. The situation should not be allowed to get to this point. Moreover, we can enter into a great contradiction: on the one hand, we ask them to do everything we tell them (we tend to infantilize them), while on the other hand, we ask them to be adults and do things for themselves. This aspect can be more complex than it may seem because there are children who, unconsciously, fear growing up and provoke infantile treatment of their parents towards them as a defense against this fear. This is what happens in the famous Peter Pan syndrome.

On the contrary, if we admit that we are not divine, that we may have to change something, and that we cannot always be right, we will be able to detect possible mistakes more easily. We will even be able to acknowledge them to our children, which will take us away from action-reaction and allow us to verify to what extent this correction has enormous healing and repairing power (infinitely more remarkable than command and control). For a parent to say to a child, *"I made a mistake," "I did not take your position into account," "I went too far," "I had a bad day and reacted in a very abrupt way," "I will see if I can do better with you,"* or *"I want us to get along better,"* will help a lot, even if we also tell them that we think that they have also gone too far. This does not happen in action-reaction-externalization-arrogance, which prevents us from thinking and rectifying. So, what example are we setting for our children so they can also jump on this bandwagon of correction and repair? Unfortunately, none.

But if we manage to encourage them to do so, we can make them see that none of us are perfect and that if we screw up, it is not in bad faith. As everyone knows, sometimes parents are so attentive that they work like *"helicopter parents,"* leaving their children without their own initiative. Or as *"snowplowing parents"* solving everything for their children. These extremes do not help much either.

Knowing this allows us to adapt and adjust during our children's development and growth, and they learn from our example, thus helping our children much more than we may think at first. Adjusting does not make us bad parents, recognizing our mistakes does not make us bad parents, apologizing does not diminish our image, and we do not lose authority in front of our children. On the contrary, it humanizes us before them, allowing us to create a climate much more conducive to dialogue, making it possible to establish tolerance within the family and, thus, enjoy the adventure of being parents and, above all, to de-dramatize.

Note

1 Throughout the book, you will observe different references to teachers, given their importance in the life of any child or adolescent, and for their usual cooperation and support in the counselling processes. These sections have been prepared and reviewed in collaboration with Professor Blanca García-Castrillón Fernández.

Reference list

Britton, R. (1998). *Belief and imagination. Explorations in psychoanalysis*. Routledge.

Hinshelwood, H. D. (1989). *Diccionario del Pensamiento Kleiniano*. Amorrortu Editores.

Horney, K. (1936). The problem of the negative therapeutic reaction. *Psychoanalytic Quarterly*, 5:29–44.

Icart, A., and Freixas, J. (2013). *La familia: Comprensión dinámica e intervenciones terapéuticas*. Ed. Herder.

Segal, H. (1982). *Introduccion a la obra de Melanie Klein*. Paidos.

Chapter 8

Adolescence unveiled

What all parents could find useful to know

Cayetano García-Castrillón and Blanca García-Castrillón Fernández[1]

One of the most notable changes detected by parents is that, as they grow older, they increasingly need to forge their identity. They seek to be treated not as small children but as adults, which means that the degree and ways of participation at home and in other areas are changing towards new ways of being and behaving, for better or worse. They will begin to demand more importance at home and school. Therefore, talking to a 6-year-old boy or girl is different from talking to a 13-year-old child.

The first thing to consider is how an adolescent reaches this stage. If everything has gone more or less well, even better, and although this is no guarantee that things will go perfectly, it indicates a good prognosis. It is also essential that the family has established the habit of talking before adolescence.

The second thing is that we can all feel a little fearful of our children's adolescence, probably because we were very reckless during that stage or because of how we experienced it in our day, and we fear that our children will do the same or go through the same thing. In addition, very often, to calm our anxiety, we demand that they behave like adults at home and like children outside. I am referring to the fact that parents, whether we want it or not, are immersed in our children's adolescence and, frequently, we suffer the anxieties that children transmit to us, or to be more precise, that they *"need"* to transmit to us, even if they shamelessly try to hide it. As a colleague of mine (Dr. Manolo Gutiérrez) says when he refers to adolescence: *"It's going to be a bumpy ride."* That is to say, adolescents often feel that their intimate space is being invaded, and their parents and sometimes their teachers feel excluded, and nobody likes this.

DOI: 10.4324/9781003581543-10

In reality, they express their degree of mental blockage in the face of the many complex challenges they face. There is no period in a person's life when there are more open issues, unknowns, questions, etc., than in adolescence. Consider that we, as parents, are used to the infantile way of relating to our children, in which they talk to us about everything very fluently. They move on to adolescence and undergo a change that can make us feel that they reject us, as I said before, and that they no longer love us. Nothing could be further from the truth. Managing so many challenges is not easy for them, nor is it easy for parents. Adolescence is not easy for any teenager. Let's look at these challenges:

Fourteen key challenges every adolescent faces

1. Accept the change in their body, whether they like the way it looks or not. In addition, the change is irreversible, which distresses them.
2. Begin to discover that their parents are not as ideal as they thought, i.e., they have to say goodbye to the parents of their childhood.
3. They say goodbye to their childhood; they no longer feel so protected in the face of life, and their parents are no longer so protective. They have to learn to defend themselves. Sometimes, unconsciously, this *"angers them"* a lot.
4. For them, turning to parents for help, advice, and support, especially at the beginning of adolescence, is synonymous with weakness, vulnerability, and lack of personality (*"Leave me alone!"*).
5. They have to be someone and have a new identity, which they will try to achieve by any means necessary.
6. They give up the idea that teachers are an extension of parents.
7. The classroom and high school become a test scenario where there are challenges to the teachers, new ways of socializing, boys and girls mix more, and academics are an imposition in which they have no say. So, every teenager has to decide whether to continue studying or not.
8. The group replaces part of the protective functions of the family, and permanent contact with them through cell phones becomes a priority.

9. They fear being just a *"creation in the image and likeness"* of adults, molded, directed, and shaped by adults. What could be better than telling an adolescent to *"do this with"* your life to ensure that they will not do it, *"of course."*

10. They are confronted by the dilemma of sex and their sexual orientation. The first sexual relations are a tremendous challenge for them; sometimes, they deny it, having sex something *"banal."*

11. They encounter the worst in human beings and must decide between destruction or construction.

12. Then they have to study—arduous work. If everything goes well, when they are 15 or seventeen, they must choose a university major or a vocation and hear that we are in a terrifying economic crisis that does not guarantee their future. Complicated, isn't it? Moreover, they feel that their successes and failures depend on them and that it is up to them to be themselves, not hybrids of their parents' and teachers' desires and aspirations.

13. Allowing themselves to be seduced by seemingly fast lanes, such as violence, drugs, etc., or to renounce them. They are confronted with the idea that making another person fail is not considered a success for them. As happens in bullying, which I call *"school terrorism."*

14. Of course, romantic letdowns, successes, infidelity, heartbreak, and disappointments in relationships sometimes being at the center of criticism, controversies, etc.

When adults are shaken by adolescent anxieties

We could say that an adolescent's planner is *"full to the brim."* All these points are critical and distressing challenges for children, and they often express them in many different ways, at junior high, at home, or high school, even producing negative impacts on teachers and families; moreover, in a truly brief time for everyone. Therefore, it is inevitable that we *"adults"* are shaken by this avalanche of anxieties that adolescents will bring to us in one way or another. And what is our reaction, in general:

1. First of all, fear, uncertainty, and the dread that everything will go down the drain, that the kids will be left without a promising future.

2. Next, we will try to diminish our fear through different methods:

   a. Increasing control over them.
   b. Systematically getting angry with them.
   c. Writing them off.
   d. Changing the way we talk to them. They are diverse types. Although they are common ways that appear occasionally, what can hint to us that we are already at the point of being overwhelmed is that they have become the usual way of relating to them. They are:

      1. Reminder mode: A teenager told me, *"My mother tires me out."* When I asked him what he was referring to, he said, *"It's the things mothers do. You know what I mean. They repeat what you already know 1,000 times as if we don't know them anymore, and we have to do them when they say; otherwise, they think we don't know them and won't do them. Things like, 'Brush your teeth, study, etc.' Don't you see that I already know! She thinks I'll forget if she doesn't tell me."* This adolescent did do those things. There are also those who do not do them and provoke this reaction in the parents, then complain and maintain an endless vicious circle of reciprocal reproaches and complaints. This latter situation is common in adolescents who, for whatever reason, are afraid to grow up.

      2. *"Wedge"* mode: This is the one in which, regardless of what is being discussed, the parents repeatedly put in *"the wedge"*: *"You have to—we give you everything—you cannot go on like this, you are always the same, etc."*

      3. *"Mute"* mode: The one where silence and uneasy calm are established at home, everyone fearing an outburst at any moment.

      4. *"Ultimatum"* mode: When parents, full of anxiety, in a last desperate attempt, resort to them: *"I will take away your cell phone for six months if you continue like this; I will not let you go out; I will take away your allowance,"* etc.

Any of these configurations express the intensity of the parents' anxiety, concern, and despair when the situation has reached a significant impasse, the *"no-way-out point"* of the conflict. What many parents are generally unaware of is that their children, like them, also suffer a lot, even though they tend to respond harshly or go into *"with-drawal"* mode, *"indifference"* mode, or *"cloistered"* mode, taking a vow of silence and, disobedience while locked their room, and also the *"explosive"* mode with intense insults and a lot of rage. All these ways of reacting are indicators that something is not working, that they have a significant conflict that is beyond them, and curiously, the more in need they are, the more difficult it is to access them. In fact, an essential part of helping parents, besides trying to understand what is going on, is to find a way to reach the child, which sometimes is not easy. Usually, adolescents do not express clearly that these situations are very distressing for them. They do not say it openly, which confuses any parent. Remember the saying: *"Tell me what you know, and I will tell you what you don't."* Surprisingly, I have observed in my daily work how all these children in the different modes I have pointed out are fully aware of the parents' reactions and how much they still care about them and deep down wish they could get closer to them. In my opinion, if you get to this point, you should seek help to get out of the impasse.

The situation can distress us so much that we overlook the most crucial thing: maintaining an open communication channel, or as open as possible. I am referring to paying particular attention when children differ, disagree, or criticize so we can ask them what their points of view are to argue, explain, and defend their positions. Sometimes, we tend not to encourage these moments because our insecurity prevents us from speaking. As Alfons Icart explains,[2] many adolescents have difficulty recognizing their difficulties to the extent that the fusion in the relationship is very marked.

Practical advice for navigating the teen years

From a practical point of view, I believe that it would be necessary to establish in schools and high schools spaces for debate directed and organized by the students to stimulate their ability to think, to discuss among themselves, and to see that things can and should be addressed. The teacher, deliberately, no longer has a relevant role in this *"hour of debate."* If there is one thing teenagers like to do, it is to discuss and feel part of a group. The advantages of the homeroom teacher being present in a respectable way are tremendous because teenagers will make them aware of their concerns, worries, etc. For them, someone close to them who knows where things are going is always a great ally.

In addition, the teacher will be able to understand much of what occurs by listening to the group's concerns. This will also help the parents, as children usually recount these experiences later at home.

Let's remember that the four most frequent questions parents ask a teenager are, firstly, *"What did you do?"* and secondly, *"Have you studied?"*, *"Have you picked up your room?"*, or *"Have you left your phone?"* In reality, it's a quest for information to put their minds at ease that things are working out. As I point out elsewhere, I think asking them how they are doing is more practical.

A minor point of clarification: it is commonplace when we hear or read someone talking about teenagers that a sense of guilt is generated, or we think of them as *"poor teenagers,"* we may even ask ourselves, *"Should we indulge them in everything because, as everyone says, they have it rough, when we think that we are giving them everything, or at least we think so?"*, *"Are teenagers the victims of adults?"*, *"Are we really that bad? Are we really doing things that badly?"*, or *"Are they just victims of their own adolescence because they also have a great time?"*

Often, more than clarifying ideas, one is left bewildered, full of doubts, and, in the worst cases, feeling a guilt that sometimes paralyzes us. Sometimes, it is not even necessary to read about the subject, but simply to listen to a parent whose different point of view disputes the truth or to a teacher with parents who find differences in their insights. I would like us to take some time to analyze these reactions in depth. One of the difficulties people generally face is walking in the dark, enduring periods of doubt, gloom, and an uncertain outcome. When we hear someone say that *"everything is self-explanatory,"* they usually omit these small but significant details: that with teenagers, nothing is evident on many occasions, and that teenagers give parents a hard time, not in bad faith, but because they do not know what they want or who they are (they are working on it) and they transmit it to us. Knowing all this serves, at least, to have more room for maneuvering with them. To give us and them a little more time.

On the other hand, it is easy to feel guilty for not knowing what to do and want to run away in a hurry from this ignorance. But the reality is that we often have no idea how to act, and that is hard to accept. And if, to top it all, we are already somewhat desperate, we try to remember how things were in our adolescence, how our parents did it with us, and we find that it is not at all similar, we panic. Rather than proceeding hastily, I think it is better to recognize that we do not know. There will be time to think about how to approach things. To do this, we must remember that pride, our own or that of others, can be a problem.

One of the ways to become seduced by pride is ignorance. Another path is through the intense anxiety provoked by situations in which we find it difficult to understand what is happening, and we rush in search of a quick solution (haste), which is more aimed at reducing the intense anxiety that presses us than resolving the conflict itself. Pride prevents the ignorant person from recognizing his own ignorance, and by ignoring it, he is hijacked by it. A covert form of pride is to judge others from a presumed possession of the truth. Getting to that point will generate many problems with a teenage son (for example: *"Son, you don't know anything about life"*). If this happens, the famous expression that refers to the biblical parable in which Jesus reproaches the hypocrites for wanting to see the speck in someone else's eye when, in fact, they do not see the plank in their own (Luke 6:39–42) comes into play. It indicates that the one who judges or criticizes has the same faults (or even to a greater degree) as those criticized by the other. A consequence of this is to treat the other as the actual possessor of the defect or the cause of the fault, which may be reassuring to the extent that one feels free of them. Still, the relationship with the other will be marked by a vicious circle that will only be broken if one sees the beam in one's own eye before judging the speck in the other's eye. If this point is reached with an adolescent child, a severe problem will arise.

As I pointed out, this parable warns of the danger of the attitudes of those who are convinced that they are far above others and only see defects in those around them. In trying to convince others of their point of view, they head down a blind alley, closed off to truth and knowledge, demanding from others, as a consequence, submission and compliance without any response or criticism whatsoever. This stereotyped model is repeated incessantly without the capacity to question it. As I pointed out before, reaching this point with an adolescent is disadvantageous.

Yet, teenagers often tell us that we, the parents, do not know anything about life, but they do. It is worth asking then: *"Have they become arrogant?"* They have, but it is a different kind of arrogance than I described before. Recognizing that they do not know something makes them feel childish, like a small child, different from the group. Curiously, they tell us that we adults do not know anything about life, that we are children. This is a clear projection of their fears

-infantile- for not knowing too much about life yet. When they relax, they can recognize what they don't know. The worrisome thing is that the adolescent's typical arrogance and the parents' arrogant reaction may come together. Then, the situation collapses. In the same way that we speak of status epilepticus or status asthmaticus as critical occurrences from the medical point of view, the *"status arrogant"* is so in the emotional field. I remember a funny anecdote of a father who told me his son kept telling him he had no idea about anything. The father lamented how the son kept cutting off his attempts to talk to him. Finally, one day, the son asked him to drive him somewhere. The father said, *"I'm good enough to be a cab driver and know how to get where he needs to go."* I told him that, in a way, his son had begun to recognize that he did know something about life, at least how to get to places. The father laughed, but I added that his son would talk to him more in the car. I thought it was a possibility because, in the car, his son was giving up his adolescent pride. The father was puzzled by my predictions, but, in the end, this is what occurred. The father asked me why I suspected that outcome. First, by agreeing to take his son, I explained that he was conveying that he did not wholly resent him for the way he spoke to him. Secondly, they could do something together, and he agreed to it on his son's proposed terms. The father said, *"So I will have to be the 'cab driver' father for a while?"* To which I replied, *"Of course."* Normally, the adolescent's pride has *"thin skin,"* and with time, it gives way. This pride has nothing to do with the *"thick-skinned"* pride that appears in highly narcissistic personalities of a destructive nature, personalities that never change nor listen, nor are they capable of recognizing any weakness, blaming others over and over, in addition to constantly feeling in possession of the truth. Fortunately, this is not common in adolescence.

Two last vital details

A small but crucial detail with teenagers is knowing that they like to decide when it's time to speak. It makes them feel that they take the initiative and are not childish. They usually do it at the most unsuspected moments: before going to bed, in the morning, at night, in short, when—as they say—they feel like it. But more deeply, it seems they let things go when they are a little less insecure and take the plunge. Of course, without it being very noticeable. They never say: *"Now, I am going to tell you what I have never dared to say before."*

Another crucial element is that parents dare to talk to their children about how they feel about life: if they are happy, if work is going well, if they are worried about something in the family, friends, etc. In other words, they should open up. For an adolescent, it is a vote of confidence to be recognized as someone capable of understanding what their parents are going through, and the typical adolescent solidarity usually appears. Rare is the teenager who refuses to support his parents if they are having a tough time. Many parents believe they will burden their teenagers; nothing could be further from the truth. Moreover, this helps teenagers see their parents as people going through various hardships in life, sometimes of a painful nature. I remember some parents lamenting that their eldest daughter spoke very badly to them, particularly the father. The father, depressed by family difficulties and the death of someone close, was suffering a lot. I asked the father if he had said this at home. He looked at me puzzled and said, *"No. That's not an option like father!"* I asked him why not. I asked him if it would hurt if his children knew about his grief. After several attempts on the father's part, he finally took the plunge. The father told me, *"There has been a lot of progress with my daughter. She is more affectionate with me and talks more. It's not that everything has changed, but this is something else."* I replied that I was pleased with his breakthrough.

Last, sometimes a boy's or girl's problems are reflected at school since that is a scenario where conflicts unfold and develop. In these cases, the scope of therapy, both with the adolescent and the parents, may fall short, and it is advisable to ask for the help of the school and the teachers. As I have already mentioned, it is common to encounter excellent collaboration, which generally proves decisive. Taking this into account and looking for an alliance with teachers will be of immense help. Often, adolescents have great trust in their teachers to whom they tell many things themselves. It's important that parents don't compete with teachers over it.

Let's take the example of an adolescent girl who, in reality, represents more of an age-related maladjustment than a pathological condition:

The Glass of Water

Clara, 15 years old, is in the waiting room in a lively chat with her mother. When I approach, Clara gets up as if to go in alone, and her mother gets up too. She looks determined not to let her mother in. She conveys that it is she who is coming and not the mother. The mother tries again to enter, too. I told the mother that, if she likes, I will see

Clara first, and then we will talk. The mother sits, a bit embarrassed, but accepts it and stays in the waiting room. I bring Clara in. She seems lively, alert, talkative, and resourceful. She looks like she has always been in therapy.

When I ask her what brings her here, she starts talking without hesitation, leans forward, and comments: *"I drown in a glass of water, make a tempest in a teapot, and I make a big deal out of anything."* I ask her to clarify it some more. She says, *"I don't know . . . For example, if I have thought about doing something and my mother tells me not to go out, that I can't go out, or that she won't let me go out, I cry. I get angry because I really like to go out. I know I should comply, but I don't. I know, but it happens."* I thought it was okay for her to stand up for herself. She tells me that she has to put up with it and has no choice but that it only happens at home, not outside, where she has many friends and gets along well with *"people."* If we look at it, she confuses complying with holding out or enduring. This confusion is commonplace in teenagers. Complying is experienced as a kind of surrender while enduring is not. Some find it difficult to differentiate one from the other. She is becoming aware of this as she compares herself with her friends. This reflects that she is capable of thinking.

I asked her what good she thought it would be for her to come here. She told me that, at first, her mother, who said she needed it, proposed it to her, but she refused. But then, she said yes to see if she could be less upset and more compliant. She tells me that with her friends, she has more patience. However, at home, she doesn't know what happens to her; she puts up with little, truly little, and that one day, she yelled at her mother and fought with her because her mother wouldn't let her watch TV and *"they had a big fight"* that day.

She is in ninth grade, and she tells me that up to sixth grade, she was doing well but then slacked off because she changed schools. Since that moment, she has had some subjects left for the summer but always passes the grade. Now, mathematics and physics are going badly.

She stresses that she starts the course well but then falls apart. *"I'm very irresponsible,"* she says. I asked her to explain why she thought that. She tells me that the teacher doesn't mark her absent if she doesn't go to school, so she doesn't go, and that this has happened more than once or twice. In addition, she tells me that in class, she thinks about what she did when she went out and what she will do. I tell her she's not even there when she's there, and she laughs. Until this year she went to class with her best friend, but this year they have been separated, they went together and talked a lot, and she thinks that this has benefited her, that before she was even more entertained than now because they talked a lot on their cell phones with *"people"* in class.

She tells me that she likes to have fun, has good friends, watches a lot of TV, uses her cell phone a lot, and doesn't do much else. She has no other hobbies. She doesn't like any sports. What she really likes is to talk with her friends. As for her future, she would like to do law, to be a lawyer, she has always liked that. She tells me that all this has happened to her since she changed to high school. Laughing, she says, *"I'm a little lazy,"* and that if it were up to her, she would be on the couch all day. If she is told to do something, she does it. She says, *"If they don't tell me to do it, I won't."* This is the typical contradiction of the adolescent. On the one hand, she asks to be let out like an adult and then induces them to tell her what to do. It is the adolescent struggle between progressing and regressing, representing the fear, in part, of growing up.

She reiterates that when she starts to study, she gets very distracted and can't keep anything in her head. She fights with her mother because she doesn't let her go out (the mother's discomfort is quite understandable). When I see the mother, she tells me that the daughter is on her cell phone too much and that she does nothing at home. The girl thinks she's not asking so much of her mother; she only asks her to go out from 5 to 10, not late at night.

Anyway, I see that she communicates well with the mother and that they talk, like in the waiting room. She has an older sister who says she talks a lot, teases her, and gets between her and her mother. But the sister gets along better with the mother than she does (that hurts the girl, it shows). Clara says she is not like her sister, who doesn't go out and sticks to her mother a lot, *"she doesn't have fun; it's her loss."* But she resents her mother's preference for her sister. And when a problem happens at home, by default, she is the one to blame (no wonder she wants to study law).

She also tells me that her mother makes her feel like she is wrong, dirty, and a hooligan for wanting to be with her friends, have fun, and go out. I ask Clara why she makes her mother stay on top of her by putting aside her studies and why she tries to make her mother see her as a child who has to be told what to do. I asked her, *"How do you want to be more independent and have more freedom, yet you do those things to send your mother the message that you can't handle the basics?"* This got Clara thinking, and she told me she hadn't thought of that. She resents her mother calling her hysterical and rowdy; she says her friends are rowdy but clarifies that they are *"good people"* (the highest grade and crucial among teenagers).

She complains again that her mother doesn't trust her, although she recognizes that she went too far last year. She was caught skipping class a few times, and she sees the mother's reaction as logical but points out that the teacher's response is not logical, as he catches her skipping and does not record an absence. This is also typical of healthy adolescents, who expect adults to call them to order and understand that they show great disinterest in them if they don't.

Working together resolved this little logjam in a brief time. Above all, once Clara understood that she was repeatedly looking for her mother to treat her like a little girl and that it was not logical for her to complain about her mother, who *"exercised her duties as a mother"* by pointing out to Clara that *"she did not fulfill her duties,"* unlike the teachers, who did not say anything when she *"missed classes."* I added that teachers do not function as fathers or mothers at their age (although it is quite frequent that adolescents expect them to do so, to exercise certain paternal or maternal functions). Clara remained pensive at this. I added that maybe she was afraid that things might not work out well for her if she decided to do what she was supposed to. She told me that this had not occurred to her, but it was possible. After a while, she told me I was right and added, *"I'd better change . . . right?"* I replied that I thought she would be glad if she did. This entire process I am describing took us about eight months of work.

Notes

1 Professor Blanca García-Castrillón Fernández reviewed this case, too, contributing from her position as an external teacher to the center where the case was developed.

2 Alfons Icart and Jordi Freixas (IPA members SEP and Fundacion Orienta, Barcelona, Spain), authors of the book *"A mi no me pasa nada"* (Nothing happens to me). In the book, they describe the difficulties of adolescents who do not recognize their difficulties and how to help them with it. Highlighting the importance of family structure.

Reference list

Aberastury, A., and Knobel, M. (1984). *La adolescencia normal. Un enfoque psicoanalitico*. Paidos.

Edgcumbe, R. (1986). Problems in the classroom: A psychoanalytic perspective on the pupil-teacher relationship. *Bulletin of the Anna Freud Centre*, 9(3):205–217.

Fernando, J. (2002). El sentimiento de culpa prestado. In *Libro anual de psicoanálisis XVI*. São Paulo-Brasil: Ed. Escuta Ltda.

Harris, M. (1983). *Se hijo de 12 a 14 años*. Paidos.

Icart, A., and Freixas, J. (2020). *A mí no me pasa nada*. Octaedro.

Torras, E. (2012). *Normalidad, psicopatología y tratamientos en niños, adolescentes y familias*. Barcelona: Ed. Octaedro.

Winnicott, D. W. (1965). *Los procesos de maduración y el ambiente facilitador*. International University Press.

Chapter 9

Building bridges

Collaborative work between parents, teachers, and psychoanalysts

Cayetano García-Castrillón Armengou
and Blanca García-Castrillón Fernández[1]

Luis is a boy between 11 and 12 years old who has always had difficulty relating to his classmates. He never really participated in his class-mates' activities. For years, Luis had a friend at school who served as a liaison in his relationships with others, helping him integrate. One day, Luis's good friend changed schools, and he found himself alone, which made his inability to relate to others very evident. Both parents and teachers noticed Luis' distressing loneliness and decided to act. Mean-while, Luis's treatment by his classmates increasingly deteriorated until he became the object of ridicule, provocations, etc. Luis began to receive psychological help to understand his relationship difficulties. In addition, his hobbies, as a lover of reading and computers, for which he had a real passion, differed from those of his classmates. His par-ents wondered (and asked the homeroom teacher) whether these were really hobbies or activities that did not involve interacting with others since they could be done alone. It was an excellent question, reflect-ing these parents' high closeness to their child and their hypotheses. We decided to do orientation work with the parents and collaborate closely with the teachers and his advisor. They all accepted, and while he continued his therapy with a colleague, I knew how Luis was doing in class and everything else the parents told me. It is crucial to collabo-rate with the teachers; they help a lot. I always tell them that they help much more than they think.

In class and at recess, the way Luis was treated as the odd one out, the outcast who could be made fun of with the acquiescence of all his classmates and with no allies to come to his defense, seemed to inten-sify. Luis suffered enormously because of this; he became depressed

DOI: 10.4324/9781003581543-11

and insisted even more on isolating himself, given how complex, cruel, and painful his relationship with his classmates was becoming. Sometimes, not many times, and especially at the beginning, the teachers' opinion was that children have always been treated this way and must learn to solve it and pull their chestnuts out of the fire (*"save their own bacon"*). This is true, but only to a certain extent. For Luis, at the moment, it was impossible.

During the review of this case, the question was raised as to why the class did not help him integrate more, that perhaps it was not only Luis who was having trouble integrating but the rest of the class as well. While we were discussing this question, we commented on a couple of incidents for which Luis was apparently responsible: two incidents of shoving classmates during recess that had ended up with them on the floor and the corresponding complaint of the *"defeated"* to the teacher for Luis' violent action, which was the subject of a reprimand. We wondered if Luis's reaction was nothing more than a response to the violent attitude to the treatment he was receiving and if the shoving was an attempt to try to get himself out of the fire.

It is very common for children to single out one of the class since if someone else is the odd one out, the rest feel safe from being the ones possibly excluded, and that is why they maintained that relationship with Luis, somewhat defensively, and that the complaints to the teacher could be an involuntary attempt to convince her that Luis, and only he, was the bad and the odd one. In response to this explanation, the teacher commented that she was struck by the fact that Luis was trying to participate more. Yet, she had the impression that they wouldn't allow him to and that he was always the one to blame for everything in the eyes of his classmates. She commented that now she understood this kind of persecutory dislike towards Luis that was causing so many headaches.

Afterward, we reflected on how to convey to the class what we had discussed, what to do, and how to do it to try to break the vicious circle that kept repeating itself. We also thought that Luis could feel so full of rage and resentment that he feared that his own internal violence would surface overwhelmingly and could truly hurt a classmate. Even though he was trying to be more involved in class, this fear of his own violence was, in turn, holding him back even more.

From all this information, we agreed to try to help Luis and the class through the following measures:

1. The teacher would acknowledge Luis's achievements more in front of the entire class, especially when he mustered the courage to participate.
2. Whenever there was an altercation in which Luis was being singled out as the *"bad guy,"* the class or those involved would talk at length about what happened.
3. A classmate should mediate these discussions on a rotating basis, including Luis himself, in the case of disputes in which he had not been involved.
4. Taking advantage of the situation for the advisor to explain that she considered it intolerable for classmates to mistreat each other, addressing the issue of bullying at length.

The basic idea was to attempt to break the vicious circle and get the class out of the *"arrogant group status"* it had established. Helping them to become aware that seeing the speck in someone else's eye and not the plank in their own is not helpful and that this group activity could help them learn to resolve their conflicts by themselves in a different way, not marked by arrogance but by discussing the conflicts that arise in the class (On one occasion, when working directly with a class of teenagers to facilitate an improvement in the relationship between them, they invented a *"conflict notebook"* in which they wrote them all down and only closed it once it had been resolved). Moreover, neither would Luis see his classmates as bad nor would they see Luis as bad. That was the objective. For this purpose, using a part of the homeroom hour, the homeroom teacher was able to connect the situations discussed with various *"existential"* aspects, avoiding the temptation to judge and prejudge hastily as a way to evade discovery, understanding and recognizing the conflicts, and thus making it possible to face them decisively with the participation of all. In a brief time, Luis changed, and so did the class.

Concurrently, the parents were informed of all these approaches. Everything improved during the six months of working together.

Note

1 Professor Blanca García-Castrillón Fernández reviewed this case, too, contributing from her position as an external teacher to the center where the case was developed.

Chapter 10

The art of discipline
Setting limits without breaking bonds

Cayetano García-Castrillón Armengou

If one thing defines a healthy child, it is their curiosity, their desire to discover and experiment with toys, tablets, balls, dolls, etc. They tend to give themselves over to it with enormous passion and become absorbed. At these moments, they often start to ignore parental requests, which is when discipline problems begin. Some kids don't listen, while others do but ignore everything. Obviously, stopping doing something that interests them enormously, and probably much more than what we tell them, is not easy for them, and they may resist by being disobedient, careless, flighty, and, to a greater degree, defiant. In other words, to stop doing something exciting and start doing something the parents ask for, which is usually not at all interesting, is a difficult transition. But doesn't this also happen to us adults? How often do we put off doing something unappetizing for another time? Well, the same thing happens to children. But we, the parents, have to maintain order, a schedule, etc. That is to say, we cannot accommodate all the children's desires, nor our own.

This is normal so far, but let us ask ourselves sincerely how we would like our children to be. It may happen that if our child is short, we would like him to be tall. If he is skilled in manual tasks, we would like him to be proficient in artistic ones. If he is good at mathematics, we would also like him to be good at language, and so on, to infinity and *"beyond."* In the worst case, we will *"compare"* him (first misunderstanding) with the little brother, the little companion who possesses *"those divine qualities"* that we sadly miss in our children. That is to say, sometimes we value them more for what they are not than for what they are. And, of course, idealistically, we would all want them to obey us on the first try.

DOI: 10.4324/9781003581543-12

If the child is doing an activity of great interest to him, it will be difficult for him to leave it. But we will have to go to bed, have dinner, brush our teeth, do homework because it is time, and say goodbye to the more entertaining activity; that is what the child is learning. It is difficult for them to obey us at first since they see little by little that not everything is possible, but when they are 5 or 6 years old, their curiosity is such that it is challenging for them. Thus, you will see that at three, they go to bed more readily than at seven, and it may seem to us that the child is increasingly disobedient, and we begin to get angry with him. He is no longer our more or less ideal child of one or two years old; he demands his autonomy from us, and some of them fight for it, which can be very tiring.

What to do? Allow it all? Evidently, *"no."* Why? If a child is allowed to do everything or is the one *"in charge,"* he will become a little tyrant, challenging, demanding, and intolerant of disappointment. When he reaches adolescence, we can already guess how he will act; it doesn't take much imagination.

But then the opposite, not allowing children anything and becoming impatient with them without further ado, would seem to be the right thing to do. Well, not so, because if we are careless, we will become tyrannical and stimulate the idea that parents are there to command and nothing else. Children will probably react by trying to avoid so many mandates in several ways, with lies, concealments, half-truths, etc., in an attempt to control us in this way. It is remarkably similar to when states use their intelligence services, and the countries spied on employ their counterintelligence methods to defend themselves. Let's say that the children use their counter-controls, their countermeasures.

You may wonder what to do. Well, the answer is to be firm. If you must go to bed, you must go to bed. If you have to do your homework, you have to do it, and so on. This does not detract from the fact that some leeway can be given. For children, these limits must be clear. But there should not be infinite limits *"to control everything";* some are enough, the scheduling of the day, what to do or not do, without becoming too obsessive (or wouldn't any of us get angry if we had to stop watching the last minutes of the Barcelona-Real Madrid match with the game tied. We would all get a little angry, honestly. So would they).

That is to say, we must be firm but know that logical resistance may appear and that resistance *"is not an attack"* on our authority as parents. In other words, we must be careful because we can mistakenly understand it as an attack against us. For this reason, it is fitting to explain to them why it is time to do something and that our demands are not to *"annoy"* them, even if sometimes it means having to stop doing something interesting. Otherwise, as I said before, we will probably become excessively strict, and the child will not understand what we say or ask. In addition, our authority increases if we explain our reasons, as opposed to the common belief that giving explanations diminishes it. Explaining is not synonymous with justifying ourselves or kowtowing to our children. This does not mean we always have to explain everything at all times because children pick it up quickly, and if everything goes well, explaining things from time to time is enough for them to collaborate and feel happy to do so.

Furthermore, this makes it easier for children to feel particular pride in seeing that they can do things that require more responsibility. The spoiled child is very unhappy because, although he apparently has everything, deep down, he feels that his parents do not trust him to be able to tolerate frustrations and to grow. Many parents understand that the demonstration of their love for their children is to give them everything.

Limits change with age: older children get more concessions, and younger children get fewer ones, although if a child is going through a grim time or is ill, it is advisable to make the limits more flexible so that they feel accepted and supported. It is striking how they remember these concessions in the future. For example, A 13-year-old girl once commented to me: *"I remember that my father took me to eat churros when they removed my cast, and I had an exam."* This never means undoing what has been achieved. Children know the special moments and understand their exceptionality, which must be clarified so that the child does not conclude that it is very profitable to be sick. Of course, the pace should not be changed on a whim.

The start of school or the return from vacation causes considerable tension, so, commonly, it seems that the discipline achieved is lost; so, at that time, it is necessary to be flexible and not rush, especially at bedtime, so that little by little, this flexibility facilitates adaptation to changes.

It is true that, sometimes, we have to be profoundly serious and firm with them, making them see that *"no"* is *"no"* and clearly explain why we take such a strong stance. Also, sometimes, we are forced to punish. However, punishments are not a magic wand, although we would like them to be.

Punishment vs guidance: The myth of the magic wand

Punishing is not bad, but some punishments are cruel or excessive. There are things that children need to know that we do not tolerate; however, excessive punishing is a symptom that something is not working or that we are getting too distressed, and we are looking for a quick, immediate, or magical change because, in one way or another, we are, or we feel, overwhelmed.

Sometimes, we believe that the permanent threat of punishment will be effective and that the child will be scared enough to stop and change, which means that not only will we forget to explain things (which does not mean apologizing for everything). We can also fall into the spiral of not talking to them and enter into a repetitive dynamic of demand-unfulfillment-punishment and absence of dialogue. If this happens, the relationship with the children will stagnate, and we will fall into the *"second misunderstanding"* in parenting: not talking. It may happen that later, in adolescence, dialogue will be much more difficult. And, sometimes, it may already be too late, requiring a lot of effort to establish a dialogue. I think that no matter what happens, talking is necessary.

But of course, when we try to talk to them, we often have to admit that our children don't make it easy for us. What else could we need: he does not obey, is not good at sports, is not as tall as his classmates, is not as good at math, does not do any homework, and looks at me with a sour face when I try to talk to him! Well, logically, we lose patience and pounce because, as I said before, neither a father nor a mother is divine (and they said that having children was a lovely experience). A child makes us go through moments of frustration. It is inevitable. There is no such thing as a divine child either.

If we end up not talking, or if we continue to trust that the magic punishment will fix everything in one fell swoop—which never happens—we will end up in despair, and we will quickly look for a *"guilty party"*: the child, the partner, friends, school, mother-in-law, etc. And at that *point*, there will be even more mental blockage.

In short, as long as another person is guilty, one is *"innocent,"* which is an advantage to freeing our conscience but a *"guarantee"* of perpetuating the situation. So, this is the *"third misunderstanding."*

We are all a little responsible for our failures and our successes. The problem is that if we get into this spiral, our heads get blocked, we do not know what to do, and, worst of all, we cannot think about what is truly happening to know what to do. It is like treating a disease without even seeing the patient or knowing what is wrong.

That is to say, in reality, there are many moments in which we do not know what to do or what is best, and if impatience invades us, how will we know which path to choose if we do not even have time to think about it, or, why not, ask the child. Any child indeed can get on our nerves, and some are very skilled in doing so.

I call the *"fourth misunderstanding"*: *"Reality does not exist."* That is, ignoring reality or realities. Let's look at a small example: A 9-year-old boy is sent to me. When I talk to his parents, they tell me that he doesn't do his homework, doesn't study, is lazy, and that, despite the punishments, nothing changes, and they don't know what to do anymore. They were pretty discouraged, desperate, and stuck.

Two days later, I was able to talk to the son, and when I asked him what was wrong, he burst into tears, telling me that his grandfather had died, that he loved him very much, and that he could not get rid of his grief. When I told him that he looked incredibly sad, he said, *"I have not been able to cry until today."* The parents were so blocked and saddened by the grandfather's death that they could not speak about it.

The *"fifth misunderstanding"* is thinking that children don't know anything or don't feel or suffer.

It can be inferred from the above that punishments shouldn't be the central axis on which we intend to get things to evolve with our children. It is important not to let punishable situations pass, and perhaps a penalty has a place and makes sense; but, if necessary, it is appropriate, in my opinion, that we do not penalize *"where it hurts our child the most,"* but that it is a constructive penalty (for example, punished to clean up the kitchen by himself for five days).

In my opinion, ongoing punishments do not have much positive influence (more so negative) on children, although there is a belief that they have a significant effect. Curiously, the children of extremely strict parents have considerable problems with resolve, while those of more permissive parents have less. The reason for this is that the stringent ones, who are all day long reminding the child what he has to do, asking him if he has done it, and reminding him of the next task, accustom the child to the idea that someone will take care of reminding him of everything and that he can *"forget,"* which makes him become a passive and inhibited child. If the parents are in control, why should he be? Others react differently by initiating, *"secretly or openly,"* a struggle in which the child sees confrontation as the only way to defend his short-lived independence and autonomy through constant defiance of the parents. Finally, some children may conclude that studies and homework are more matters of parental interest and do not affect them firsthand. Worst of all, they may *"obey"* only to please their parents. Also, they may give up in the face of the immense number of demands that overwhelm them. A degree of permissiveness allows children to take their own responsibility in a more parent-friendly manner. Sometimes, parents can have a hard time reducing their level of control because of the threat that everything will fall apart.

It is easy for parents to be very demanding when we compare our children with others or when we want them to be the expression and manifestation of our success. There comes the point when we use them to *"show off"* how good we are at everything, including our role as parents. Thus, we become not parents at the service of the children, but instead, they are at the service of our *"narcissistic"* interests. Over time, this leads to an outbreak of confrontations. The adolescent must prove that *"his"* way of feeling has its own identity by rejecting what is demanded because he understands that he is being asked to succeed, not by himself, but by his parents. This usually ends badly if the following *"inversion"* occurs: *"If I fail, my parents don't succeed; I do. Thus, my failure is at the same time my success."* Reaching this point represents a tremendous disaster.

This leads us to the *"sixth misunderstanding,"* which would be to despise and insult the children: *"You are worthless, you are useless."* This, in addition to depressing the children because they feel that they are continually letting their parents down, generates enormous anger in them because of the humiliation they have received. If parents demand important levels of goodness from their children, the children, perceiving them as unattainable, may completely renounce the good and take a worrying turn towards the hostile, the violent, and the aggressive in an incredibly impulsive and excessive way.

Children learn not only from what they hear from their parents but also from their behavior. Thus, a child who is hit and punished frequently may hit his peers. After all, *"That's what mom or dad does."* That is to say, without realizing it, sometimes parents endorse, through our behavior, the behaviors children repeat at school, and we immediately censure them.

"Seventh misunderstanding": *"As we are your parents, we always get it right, we have that gift. . . . You, my son, have the gift of failing."* It provokes a lot of anger in children when parents do not admit any

mistakes, even when they show them to us with the clarity that a child or adolescent usually has. Locking ourselves in the idea that we are always right greatly irritates children because they understand that we are not interested in their opinions, reasons, or arguments.

"Eighth misunderstanding": Separations. Specifically, there is a lack of knowledge of how much children suffer or come to suffer. Recently, a teacher told me that a brilliant 8-year-old student of hers, who could barely answer the questions on a test, was crying in class because of his parents' separation. Sometimes, separating parents feel so guilty that they tend to alleviate their guilt by *"accusing"* the other parent. Occasionally, they use their children to do so. There is nothing more distressing than this for a child who sees their parents, who are separating, fighting. I am convinced that, in many cases, if parents were aware of this, it would greatly ease the tensions of separation.

Using the child can be one of the most frightening aspects of separation. For example, when children are consciously or unconsciously used as a tool for hatred, resentment, and revenge against the parent who has left. Or when one or both parents perpetuate an attitude of hostility and resentment towards the other, involving the children by encouraging them to verbalize their hatred and then enjoy it. Too, when one of the parents tries to explain the causes of their separation to the child by arguing the cruelties and intolerance of the other. For me, it is clear parental negligence that causes a profound traumatic impact on children. These parents should be helped to understand that putting aside the narcissistic wounds generated by separation is the best thing they can do for their children.

If the above examples occur, the son is knocked about by one and the other. He is forced to hate others, with which his structures and personality become shattered, and, unfortunately, he ends up falling into a deep depression that no one stopped to consider. But children are the ones who pay the highest price. Let alone if they are forced to testify in court. In these cases, panic and anxiety crises and depressive and phobic reactions are frequent. Confusion usually floods the children who find themselves with parents who have not been able, have not known how, or have not wanted to settle things in a sensible and civilized way. Even sometimes, after the trials, the *"battles"* continue with more complaints for not paying alimony, etc. One often thinks, *"poor children,"* because who can help them in those situations? It is not uncommon for one parent to seek help for the child, and the other parent refuses. Honestly, as I said before, if parents who were with each other knew the pain they cause, many would not do it. Sure, their child getting leukemia would stop bickering, but they should be aware that it causes emotional leukemia in them.

Managing sibling rivalries constructively

Should parents intervene in their children's disputes or leave them to see if they can fix the situation themselves? That they can fix it by themselves is clear. But, when one of the siblings approaches the threshold of physical or emotional cruelty, parents should intervene by setting limits.

Let's look at a practical case: Pablo and Alejandro are two brothers who love soccer and often play against each other. Pablo, the older one, is usually also the referee, which Alejandro, the younger one, doesn't mind. One day, Pablo, more angry than usual, according to his father, told Alejandro that everything was a foul and that the ball was for him because of the fouls committed. Alejandro started to get fed up when he saw that he never got to shoot the ball and said something about it to Pablo, who replied, *"You shut up and do what I say. That's why I'm the referee."* Alejandro got angry and did not accept it, and Pablo kicked him. When his father, who had seen the situation coming, reached them, Pablo kicked Alejandro again, yelled at him, and told him to shut up. Pablo was angry and out of control, which was rare for him. The father, who acted as a *"good referee,"* took the ball away from Pablo and stopped the mistreatment of Alejandro.

Pablo could not overcome his irritation, and his father punished him by sending him to his room. At dinnertime, Pablo, of course, did not come. At bedtime, he would not go to sleep; he played alone in his room with an undeniably defiant and provocative attitude. The mother realized he was trying to provoke them and did not say anything. With his defiant and thoughtless attitude, Pablo was trying to make the parents lash out against him and, in that way, *"erase"* the fact that he had lashed out against the brother harshly and excessively. Pablo would not give in, nor would he come to his senses. And that is how they went to sleep. After a while, Pablo, who had not spoken up to that moment, went to his parents' room to tell them he could not sleep and was afraid. In my opinion, not surprisingly, because one of the most frequent reasons for transient insomnia is not having a clear conscience, and Pablo did not have one. I suppose that Pablo's fear came from being aware of his violent outburst. He was also taking another *"tone."* Pablo embraced his parents. They allowed him to do so, and later, well into the night, they talked about what had happened. The parents explained to him, the father in this case, that parents cannot let siblings hurt each other and that he thought that, rather than playing soccer, he was looking for a fight, or so it seemed because, at other times, when they played, he did not behave like that. The parents asked him to apologize to his brother the next day, and finally, Pablo could go to sleep.

It is imperative to understand how sometimes children push us to behave with them in a way we usually would not. Children often do this, and then, without realizing it, they are the ones directing us. All we perceive is that they are attacking us, and we respond to their attack without further ado. Pablo's parents restrained themselves; moreover, when he went to the room, they offered him a way out to *"clean up the situation"* instead of scolding him again and sending him to his room, which we impulsively want to do. In addition, Pablo's parents talked to him about what had happened, encouraging the habit of solving problems not by imposition but by talking and showing him that if you have to apologize, you have to, period.

Another brief example: Loreto is a hard-working mother. One day, while making dinner, her daughter, also named Loreto, tells her that she will not have dinner. Half an hour later, the daughter says she wants dinner. The mother, who had already cleaned up the kitchen, yells at her, *"You're not getting dinner anymore, I'm done for the day . . . shit."* The sisters told the mother that she had gone too far. Loreto's daughter left crying and saying that she had no appetite before, but now she did. After a while, the mother apologized and explained that she was exhausted. She told her daughter that moms can't handle everything (which is true and obvious) and that she should prepare something for herself if she wanted to have dinner. Loreto ate her dinner. The mother's ability to recognize that she crossed the line fixed the situation and smoothed the way. It will make it easier for her daughter to recognize her own overreaching in the future. It is usual for children to get cranky when they are hungry or tired. Excessive tiredness or excitement may even make it difficult for them to sleep, or they may not realize they are hungry or sleepy.

Of course, we parents worry a lot about whether we are excessively rigid or permissive. Every family has its own style, rules, and discipline, without which we would not have maturing children but big babies. However, when we put these into practice, we will encounter a lot of opposition and have to repeat things often: teeth, room, study, etc. This type of opposition is standard at this age and will require patience. However, totally adapting ourselves to the child is a risk, but the opposite can also be a risk. It does not mean that sometimes we should not suspend the rules (birthdays, achievements, illness, etc.).

The *"last misunderstanding,"* and curiously the most common, is that we do not know how to recognize the *"good things"* about our children, and we forget to tell them. I do not give examples because, as soon as one remembers, one realizes what we did not say or value. It seems to me a significant error to consider that the good things should not be highlighted on the basis that a child has done *"what he had to do and was supposed to do"* and that, therefore, little or nothing should be praised, as would be the case of the child who passes at the end of the course and the parent says: *"I'm not going to congratulate you because it is what you were supposed to do,"* belittling the merit for the achievement. This is one of the things that most depresses a child.

As a final summary, discipline should not consist of *"taming the child"* through endless punishments and demands, with which the only thing we would achieve is either a latent rebelliousness that will surface in adolescence or obedience and submissiveness that will risk their children becoming easy prey for others throughout their lives. Part of children's growth includes rebelliousness, which is an attempt to differentiate themselves, to be noticed, and, sometimes, to expose their points of view of what parents do, and, why not, admit it, sometimes they are right when they make us see our *"mistakes."* Resorting to continuous threats or systematically saying, *"When dad comes, you will find out,"* or something similar only serves to make false fixes. The worst thing is that, implicitly, we are indicating that threatening is a good option to solve the conflicts (later in adolescence, they may also resort to the threat as a way of fixing things). On the other hand, standing firm, dialoguing, explaining, and showing great patience allows children to differentiate between right and wrong, allowing them to rectify things on their own gradually. It is understood that this prevents many problems due to a lack of dialogue in future adolescence.

The commented cases show the joint work through which parents could not get entangled in the immediate or in the reactions that children usually provoke in different daily situations.

Some of the following questions are useful for repositioning ourselves as parents. They are not taken from a scientific questionnaire. They are routine questions but can also be helpful: What was my child's last worry? When was the last time I talked to him or her? What makes them most angry, and what does he or she like the most? Can you describe the way he/she is? Do I acknowledge his/her achievements? Have I ever apologized to them? Have I ever agreed with him/her, or have I never agreed with them? Do I hold back my affectionate gestures with him/her, or do I show them? How many times have I blamed my partner for what happened?

Celebrating what works: The victories of parenting

Finally, it is also imperative for parents to observe the amount of success they have with their children. Many times, they are not aware of what they have achieved. They can help their children grow and mature and strengthen their abilities. Many parents believe that they have done everything wrong. Nothing could be further from the truth. This happens because they feel excessively guilty about what they have not yet been able to do. Let's look at one last example:

In the first post-summer visit of parents I have been working with for more than a year, they tell me that everything has somewhat improved with their fourteen-year-old son. During this period, two things caught their attention. One was that while they were traveling in the car, the engine light came on, the engine slowed down, and their son, who loves mechanics, became terrified and overly excited and shouted, *"Stop, stop!"* The parents were struck by the intensity of their son's anxiety. Finally, they told him to calm down and that they would turn around and take the car to the repair shop. It was a difficult incident. The parents insisted upon his extreme reaction. I thought it was the son's reaction to the risk of complete catastrophe, somehow reflecting his own difficulties. When I started working with these parents, they told me that their son avoided everything, did not do any activities, did not go out, and was barely keeping up with his studies. In addition, on numerous occasions, he flatly refused to leave the house. These difficulties, which are so important, are being resolved. During that initial period of treatment, his parents were always scolding him, telling him the behavior couldn't continue and that he was putting his future at significant risk.

One of the results of working with them is that they stopped pressuring him because we saw that this ended up distressing everyone. In a way, the parents' de-dramatization helped them to convey to him that those problems, including engine problems, can be fixed.

The second issue they commented on was how their son could not stand being around his cousin of the same age because she is always telling him what to do in a domineering manner. But for the parents, it was striking to see how he did not want to jump through hoops. I showed them that, far from accepting this submissive way of relating to his cousin, he preferred to stand up for himself. In fact, it was a step forward for the son as he had always been passive and let himself be *"dragged along"* by others. They completed their comments by telling me that the son did nothing when he was back home and before starting the school year; he played video games for hours, got up late, and did not seem to get out of this cycle. The mother got angry with him. She told me: *"I don't know if I have done right or wrong. I took the gaming console away from him. I told him that this can't be. He has to do his things, read, do his homework, etc. In the end, I got angry. Also, I stopped talking to him because he wouldn't listen to reason, and I told him I was going to the tennis club and that he would have to figure out what he would do."*

The mother thought she had overdone it. But she was surprised when her son called her, after a while, as if nothing had happened to tell her he was getting ready and going to the club. Then, the parents insisted that he had better read. So, the son found a book by a famous athlete who had gone through emotional difficulties and sought help so it would not interfere with his successful professional career. The parents told me that the son feels the athlete is his idol. I added that he could possibly identify with the idea that emotional difficulties are not catastrophic, that they can be treated—the son has also started therapy—and that he has identified with the athlete in some way.

The mother reiterated her concern that she had overdone it. I told her that she saw that her son was stuck and intervened, stopping that situation like the son asking them to stop the car. She stopped his video gaming, and by going to the club, she also stopped getting into long and fruitless arguments with her son. That is what I explained to her. In passing, I told them it might be helpful to explain it to their son in a later incident—that, as parents, they also react if they see that something is not working. She saw *"the warning light on"* in that situation and did not allow *"the light to stay on."* I thought their son was able to identify that parents are *"also"* aware of the inner workings at home, as important as being aware of those of the car, like his son said.

In other words, this mother didn't think she was right as she really was. Parents often know more than they believe. Finally, a little sense of humor at home benefits everyone.

Reference list

Farber, B. A., and Nevas, D. (2001). Parents' perceptions of the effects of their child's therapy. *Journal of the American Academy of Psychoanalysis and Dynamic Psychiatry*, 29(2):319–330.

Ferenzi, S. (1933). Relaxation and education. In *Final contributions to problems and the methods of psychoanalysis*. London: Hogarth Press (1955).

Freud, S. (1937). Constructions in analysis. In *The standard edition of the complete works of Sigmund Freud*, Vol. XXIII. London: Hogarth Press (1950–74).

Furman, E. (1957). Treatment of under-fives by way of their parents. *Psychoanalytic Study of the Child*, 12:250–262.

Jacobs, L. (ed.) (2008). *Parent-centered child therapy: Attachment, identification, and reflective functions*. Lanham, MD: Jason Aronson.

Klein, M. (1952). On observing the behavior of young infants. In R. Money-Kyrle, B. Joseph, E. O'Shaughnessy and H. Segal (eds.), *The writings of Melanie Klein*, Vol. III. London: Hogarth Press (1975).

Lassers, E., and Lassers, W. J. (1985). Children and parents in the divorce court. *American Journal of Psychoanalysis*, 45:77–79.

Meltzer, D. (1975). Adhesive identification. *Contemporary Psychoanalysis*, 11:289.

Novick, K., and Novick, J. (2019). *Trabajo con padres y terapia con hijos*. Ed. Herder.

Chapter 11

When parents disagree

Turning conflict into strength

Cayetano García-Castrillón Armengou

One of the most frequent reactions among parents when tensions exist, especially during their children's adolescence, is to accuse the other of being *"wrong."* That is, either the father or the mother questions the behavior of the other. Thus, one undermines the other, sometimes even in front of the son or daughter. This situation enrages the *"overruled"* person, which generates considerable resentment within the couple. In the extreme, it can lead to a rift in the relationship, which can end in a breakup or a request to the person being overruled to shut up, accusing them of making things worse. Sometimes, one parent expects the other parent to behave in the same way as them (cloning). It is rather challenging to reach a complete agreement in a couple in conflict situations, mainly because a child does not establish the same type of relationship with his father as with his mother; there are nuances between the two, and this is often forgotten.

Each parent reacts differently. For example, a father may scold more often than a mother, or vice versa; one may be more permissive than the other, give different importance to the same issue, etc., which is normal. Thus, when one partner expects the same type of response to the child from the other as an indicator of collaboration and mutual understanding, they may be disappointed.

Parents can ease this tension by talking calmly and in private about their diverse ways of reacting, clarifying very well why one responds differently from the other, and understanding that diverse ways of reacting are not a betrayal of the other. In addition, children understand their father and mother have distinct personalities and reactions and do not expect the same from both. This does not mean that a child will turn to one parent to tell them that the other parent is wrong or that

DOI: 10.4324/9781003581543-13

there is a significant disagreement at some point. And if they do, they may be just looking to be proved right. Although, on most occasions, children seek mediation. For example: *"Dad, Mom only lets me go out until 2 o'clock, and I want more,"* or *"Mom, Dad won't let me,"* or: *"Mom, Dad told me that . . ."*

Conveying to the children that you will talk to mom or dad is particularly important because it prevents them from seeing, as the only option for resolving the situation, allying themselves with the parent more favorably inclined to their wishes. If this does not happen, the children may *"take advantage"* of the discrepancy, which can block the situation and cause the parents, instead of facing the problem with the child, to *"argue"* among themselves. In addition, the child is not given the option of proposing a consensus-based solution—to clarify, it is as if a child were to simply transfer the situation to their parents and withdraw from the matter, as if to say, *"There you go, understand each other, and I'll wait."* In other words, *"It's good fishing in troubled waters."*

However, in these situations, there is little gain in the end. Teenagers, or the youngest ones, do not do it to manipulate but rather because facing relationship conflicts at home is difficult. As I pointed out, it is easier to avoid getting into this spiral if the parents convey that they will talk about it among themselves and then tell the child their thoughts so that they can discuss it with the child and ask them what options they propose. If the parents still do not agree, that is okay. Telling a child that there are differing opinions is not a negative thing and that, this time, what one parent says, and not the other, will be done because one of them is doubtful and the reasons for the doubt. For example: *"Look, I don't think it's right for your mother to let you go out for so long because I think it's too much, but I think her criteria are more reasonable, although I don't agree."* This allows a child to know the point of view and concerns of the parent who disagrees and may have the opportunity to *"show, explain, discuss"* that nothing is wrong. This removes the tempting idea that children and adolescents have of their parents always being *"as they want them to be"* and not as they are. That is, different in the same way that each child is different.

However, if the tensions in the couple still do not dissipate, it is advisable to seek help. The presence of a third party can help to explore and understand what is happening. Most often, one of the parents is entirely convinced that the other is *"screwing things up,"* which blocks communication. Throughout my experience, I have observed something very peculiar. Many times, it is true that the other is mistaken, but the one who is *"right"* does not see that they are also messing up by accusing the other. I suppose you all remember examples of disagreements that you have resolved.

I must clarify that when I refer to the father or mother, I am referring to maternal and paternal functions. In couples where both members are of the same gender, the functioning is identical.

Reference list

García-Castrillón, C. (2007). *Ser padres, ¿una misión imposible?* Glosa.

Morgan, M. (2020). Being a couple and developing the capacity for creative parenting: A psychoanalytic perspective. *Journal of Child Psychotherapy*, 46:191–205.

Chapter 12

Family 3.0

Parenting in the digital age

Cayetano García-Castrillón Armengou

I often wonder, and I ask parents, *"How many times a day do they use the words 'cell phone' at home?"* It is a valid and practical indicator of the role of the cell phone in family life. For example, phrases such as: *"Put the cell phone away!", "Are you still on your cell phone?", "I'm going to take your cell phone away,"* etc., are uttered repeatedly. The fact that the cell phone has become a main character in family life since family digitalization, as I call it, is undeniable.

The cell phone gives the entire family unprecedented accessibility to everything to an extent previously unknown, including contacts, acquaintances or strangers, personal information, social networks, shopping, and information of all kinds. This availability generates the powerful expectation that everything is immediately at hand, accessible, and possible. I call this phenomenon the *"enabling of desire."* In other words, it is possible to satisfy any desire without effort, or at least without the work required in the non-virtual world for attainment or achievement. The *"digital offering"* is downright tempting. Obviously, the mind associates this, at least in the first instance, with no cost, let's say, *"zero cost"* . . . apparently.

The risk of this *"desire enabling"* taking hold is that it confuses our children regarding how things are achieved in life. This makes it necessary and desirable for parents to plan and manage the cell phone's entry into their children's lives. Simply leaving it to them is too presumptuous, or at the very least risky, in the same way that no parent would leave their car to a child or bring a puppy home without any planning.

This opens up an area that I call *"family technology management."* Simply put, *"not everything goes,"* as in any other management we do

DOI: 10.4324/9781003581543-14

in our lives. I break this management into four sections: the when, the how much, the what, and the why. Let's look at them:

1. **When**

   In my experience, it is not at all suitable to have access to a cell phone before age 10, and if it is later, even better. In adolescence, it is unavoidable from the age of 12. In any case, and being realistic, it is impossible for a child under ten not to use a cell phone. I think it is an excellent time to explain to them, as a preventive measure, that its use has a time limit and that they should never use it without parental supervision. This avoids many unpleasant surprises. Supervision is complicated because, realistically speaking, parents are not going to be by the child's side all the time, so the best thing to do is to limit the content they can access.

2. **How much**

   As I stated, it should be made clear to children from an early age that they do not have unlimited use of their cell phones. And that, at lunch, dinner, at night, or during family time, its use is not authorized, both for them and us (it is essential to practice what you preach). This approach paves the way for them to understand these reasonable limits by the time they reach adolescence. If we begin to propose limits in adolescence, it is already a little late. It will be much more difficult for children to understand, especially if, when they are young, we give them a cell phone at family gatherings or with friends so that they *"do not bother us."* When they grow up, they will say, *"Give me the cell phone, and I won't bother you. Isn't that how things used to be?"* I imagine you get the picture.

3. **What**

   As I pointed out, at an early age, it is imperative to try to control the content. However, it is also essential to foresee the future by explaining to them that everything that appears on the internet may seem true, but it is not necessarily true. Thus, we can explain to them that, in the future, on social networks, they will see that everyone is happy, beautiful, gorgeous, hilarious, fabulous, etc. We must make it clear to them that this reality is usually retouched, which will help them to have a critical view of the content they see. That is to say, to promote critical thinking in children. We will also tell them not to trust strangers, not to give out family information, not to agree to do what they are suddenly asked to on the screen, not to put up photos of themselves, and if they receive accusations or criticism (as happens in WhatsApp groups in schools, which are widely used in bullying), not to be afraid to tell someone. In the same way that we teach them how to cross the street or ride a bike, we must help them to know how to navigate the internet. To do so, we don't need to be very insistent; if we start early, we can discuss these issues little by little.

4. **Why**

As children, it is easier for them to leave their cell phones behind than when they are teenagers. In adolescence, it is more complicated because it is as if they have a *"gang"* at home all the time through social networks. They experience it as *"I'm left out, not knowing what's happening with people if I'm not keeping up on my cell phone."* Interrupting contact is experienced as being excluded from the gang and makes them incredibly nervous. But, it is worth explaining that it is particularly important to maintain communication in the family because that is when everyone will be able to know how things are going, comment on how the day went, etc. Therefore, time with the mobile phone is not unlimited. Let us remember that the more a family talks, the better everything will be. All children understand this, even if it is difficult for them. And above all, limiting the use of mobile phones is not an arbitrary imposition. There are so many powerful reasons to limit it.

A tremendously striking question is why the awareness of the passage of time is altered with the use of the mobile phone. One day, a teenager told me that the hours were passing, and it seemed to her that not so much time had passed. While we were talking, she told me that she thought it was because of how quickly the content appeared on the networks. That, she believed in this way, there was no time to perceive time. She told me she thought that was *"the big social media trick"* and told me that *"it was as if you ate your favorite food all the time, but that you don't feel that you are full."* And that there was another, always put about the things you like. Then I said: *"Like your favorite food?"* She said: *"Yes, yes."* This young teenager was absolutely right. I think that, as this teenager says, showing children the *"tricks of the internet"* would help a lot.

This *"unconscious consumption of time"* produces a chain effect: there is no time to study, do other things, etc. I suppose you parents do know very well what I am talking about.

Cell phone overuse as addiction and emotional refuge

The question causing the most worry is whether cell phone use is excessive or if our child is addicted to the cell phone. I am going to expand on this point a little more. To know if a boy or a girl is a potential candidate to become addicted to the cell phone, there are two key factors to consider. One is their degree of frustration and tolerance. Having the capacity to tolerate frustration will protect them from this risk to the same degree as cell phones since some games and applications *"slyly"* provide immediate satisfaction to the user, making them feel that *"no frustration"* is possible.

You may wonder how we parents can help our children cope in the best possible way with the countless frustrations that life inevitably throws at us. Let's see, the child, since birth, is *"losing things little by little"*: first weaning, now no longer sleeping in the parents' room, then exchanging the bottle for the spoon, then maybe having a little brother, then going to kindergarten, and no longer being at home, etc., etc., etc. For the child, all these changes mean a loss of what came before and a transitory period during which they have not had enough time to *"enjoy and savor the advantages of what is new versus what is left behind."* In other words, there are many moments of associated and simultaneous loss and frustration. Suppose we do not make transitions suddenly; for example, we alternate a little breast and bottle feeding, go to daycare for a shorter time in the beginning, and have more time together at bedtime because they need time to get used to it and require this in those moments, etc. We will make our child feel that frustration is not so painfully dramatic, nor a painful loss, nor an unbearable emptiness, and that, despite everything, moving forward has its advantages.

The second key factor is if, on the contrary, we act in a hurry, abruptly and hastily, the child will experience the loss as something very upsetting, as something good that has been taken away from him all at once. This impression can be established at a very early age. If this happens, children become hyper-demanding, exacting, and intolerant of any frustration or disappointment, laying the foundation for the future in which cell phones, drugs, games, and alcohol provide immediate satisfaction with no waiting. Today, online gambling represents a great danger in this regard.

Another factor to be careful with is making our sons or daughters accustomed to getting everything they ask for. Sometimes, this happens because we understand that we show them *"how much we love them"* through this incredible generosity. But they will not understand it that way. They can get confused and become tyrants because we have made them believe that we must keep giving them everything they ask for.

So, a child with no tolerance for frustration and with tyrannical traits in his behavior is an excellent candidate for addiction. It goes without saying that if a child, due to life circumstances, has not felt wanted, loved, appreciated, and welcomed, it will impact them so much. They will desperately look for anything to relieve that unbearable feeling of loneliness. It is a fundamental antidote to show them our affection, express it, and embrace them. There is nothing more powerful than feeling loved to avoid falling into addictions. For professionals, it is a significant challenge to be able to detect childhood depression because, if not, it leaves deep emotional after-effects in the future, among them the ones I have just described.

Generally, if the previous problems do not exist, it is typical to overuse the cell phone in excess. Or, in times of anxiety or stress, it is occasionally used as a sedative. Parents can easily see this. For example, *"Now they are on it more hours than before,"* etc. We get a sense that the issue is only the cell phone overuse when it is relatively easy to regulate the situation. However, if real battles break out regarding limiting use, it is reasonable to think that significant underlying conflicts exist.

As I pointed out earlier, cell phones are sometimes an escape route: for example, the shy child who finds it easier to connect through the cell phone than directly or the depressed child who plays the same game repeatedly to feel that something is going well. In these cases, the worrying thing would be to neglect the underlying emotional problem. These situations do not correspond to addiction, nor to simple overuse, but to the use of the cell phone *"as a refuge."* Thus, evasive or compensatory use takes hold in the face of conflict. This is why assessing the possible presence of emotional difficulties is vital so that the cell phone does not become a permanent refuge two brief examples:

Michael, 17 years old, played the same game for hours and hours, enjoyed it and was good at it. When I asked him why he did it, he told me *"at least I do something right"*. A clear example of refuge from the total distrust of being able to achieve things in his life. Or Lucas who played for hours and hours, until he got bored when he commented to me *"that's how I beat everyone"*. In a clear desire to feed their need to succeed at all costs. But if the idea had been instilled in them that *"only"* the cell phone would bring them relief, what started as a refuge would have ended up as an addiction. This explains why using the cell phone is often an attempt to find a way out. If excessive use is observed, it is worth questioning and investigating whether something painful has happened or whether there is an underlying conflict.

Overuse is common because children have not pondered what they can do *"without the cell phone."* Let me share an anecdote. The baker I went to once told me that he got angry with his son and restricted his cell phone use after a particular hour. The boy told him he would be bored, and my baker said, *"Well, then you'll be bored."* Surprised, the baker replied to me that his son had learned origami and that he was phenomenal, a pleasant surprise for both of them because the son did not even suspect that he could like that.

This anecdote is more relevant than it seems because, many times, we parents feel guilty that our children are bored. But if they do get bored, as in this case, they may look for something to do to stop being bored if their cell phone isn't available. In short, *"boredom is not a bad thing."*

Another aspect that surprised me is when teenagers tell me they will be very strict with cell phone schedules when they become parents. They are perfectly aware of their excesses. Another thing is that it is difficult for them to limit themselves or to accept limits being placed on them. And when I ask them why they don't limit their use, since they say that when they become parents, they will. Some of them said to me: *"I am not a father yet."*[1]

Social validation: Chasing followers and *"likes"*

Indeed, who doesn't like to be followed or *"liked"*? For teenagers, especially, it is a barometer of their social prosperity or lack thereof. It is a way to feel important, recognized, and valued. In general, I see this point as reasonable at those ages (there may be particular situations where the kids' desire reaches obsessive levels, but it is not what I have observed in my usual practice). Strikingly, boys or girls with a significant number of *"likes"* on social networks are subject to countless insults, criticisms, hateful, derogatory, and sometimes threatening comments. Hidden by anonymity and caused by destructive and reactive envy to *"likes"* or the *"sale"* of an idealized image of themselves. This takes its toll on many of them. It goes without saying that the *"predators on social networks"* capture these boys or girls who are excessively in need of *"likes."* The tactic they use is to flatter the adolescent eagerness for appreciation and, subsequently, to subject them to significant blackmail, hence the importance of warning them of the risk of contacting strangers, even more so if they *"butter them up."* I believe that it is necessary to explain it to adolescents and children the same way that when they are young, we explain to them not to go with strangers no matter how much they say: *"We know your parents,"* *"I have a present for you at my house,"* *"Don't be afraid of me and come with me,"* etc. We should also explain the same thing about social networks to our children.

As I said before, it is imperative to explain to them from an early age that not everything is as wonderful as it seems on the internet. The value of *"being looked at or admired"* by everyone and of showing off all (that is measured by the number of *"likes"*) can become a problem. In this way, we can instill in the adolescent that to *"be someone in this life"* appearing constantly on social networks is unnecessary. In other words, in everyday life, *"it is not worth it, nor does it sell."* This idealization of the every day, which, in my opinion, is the *"climate in the social networks,"* can make the adolescent believe that he leads a miserable life, to the extent that he compares his daily reality with the virtual one, not to mention if he compares himself with others and their virtual lives.

Let's look at another example. After the summer and several months of working together in therapy for a substantial academic block during which he had not studied for a year due to severe bullying, William, 16 years old, tells me that he is better but realized that he has refused to go to the pool and the beach even though everyone else was going. He explains that it is because of his stomach. William is athletic and regularly goes to the gym. In other words, he doesn't have a big belly. But he tells me that he realizes this is strange, but he is unhappy with his belly. He explains that it is not in a state where it is fit to be seen and that this has held him back. Logically, I asked him how his stomach would have to look to go to the pool or the beach. He answers, *"More toned."* But he realizes that 95% of people don't have that ideal stomach, and 5% do. I question further whether he wants the perfect stomach or if he's caught up in the idea of the perfect stomach seen on social media. He answers me that he understands that 95% of people don't have an ideal belly but that inside, he also thinks that it is the other way around, that 95% have a perfect belly and 5% don't. I tell him that it is clear that this second criterion has guided him and that, therefore, if he goes to the beach, he will draw negative attention as one of the 5% with an unacceptable belly. I tell him that it sounds to me like the influence of social media, which continually presents perfect but false images.

His answers are priceless. They were as follows: *I think that from seeing so much, I formed an idealized picture, and of course, I compare myself to others, and I come out looking bad.* I let him know that I agreed with him. However, he does not understand why he believes that unreality. He knows it, but at the same time, he's trapped in it. I could only tell him that it was an excellent question, that I, at least for the moment, did not know how to answer it, and that I had better think about it. Then he told me,

> *Cayetano, cell phones listen to everything and control what you look at on the internet, and then they bombard you with the topics you have looked at. I think that there comes a time when images of the stomachs of athletic people appear the most, so it seems that this is the norm and not what one thinks.*

My response was that I hadn't heard a better explanation from anyone about how the bombardment on the internet alters the perception of what is normal. I simply added, *"It creates an inverted reality."* He agreed and said he doesn't understand why people lie so much. After all, it is people who run the internet. But I asked him, *"Do you think that, despite knowing it, one can fall into believing those lies?"* He said yes, and I asked him why. He told me that he did not know or could not think of anything, to which I replied, *"Well, I have come up with an idea; let's see what you think. This is my hypothesis: Greed."*

He remained thoughtful. Then I told him I believe this bombardment, a falsehood that can induce idealization of and believing it because it stimulates the fantasy that this is how one will triumph socially, be the best, and have continuous success. And that emotionally, it can be so tempting that, in spite of detecting what we mentioned earlier, this temptation catches us. William's answer was, *"That's for sure."* I am still thinking why the word greed occurred to me. Is it emotional greed? I don't know. As I discussed with him, I do know that Willian's search for emotional security made it easier for him to fall into that trap. Far from diminishing his insecurity, it held him back and increased his insecurity at the risk of becoming obsessed with the subject.

On the other hand, it doesn't take much imagination to think of the consequences and what can happen if the bombardment is cyberbullying.

In addition, I think this background is essential for parents to know so that they can explain it to their children to prevent future complications.

This exceptional intervention with Willian allowed us to see the psychological mechanisms that social media activates or can activate, obviously, also in adults.

In general, it can happen that if the desire for things to be fixed immediately is intense and the person finds the *"great solutions"* on the internet, this *"binomial"* is intensely consolidated. I call it: *"the dancing couple."*

On the other hand, sometimes they serve as a good means of communication in the family, and sometimes, they allow children to talk about what they do not say directly. It is frequent that, after an argument at home, contact is reestablished *"as if nothing had happened"* through WhatsApp. However, it has its limitations. The most important thing to remember is *"Do not write in the heat of the moment via WhatsApp."* Many children or parents have regretted *a posteriori* not having restrained themselves.

Finally, a child with problems can always become excessively hooked on the cell phone, which is a *"warning sign."* In fact, prohibiting its use is parents' most frequent decision in conflict situations, believing that the cell phone is the only problem. But when they do, in most cases, the problem remains. Therefore, to my understanding, if there is a concern about excessive cell phone use, it is worth exploring in depth how things are going in that child's life because something is undoubtedly wrong. The cell phone, its overuse, addictive use, or use as a refuge are some of the most apparent symptoms.

It is clear that sometimes, parents also have to regulate their use of cell phones. It never hurts to lead by example. Children often say, *"You don't stop with your cell phone, either."* How often are they right? To be honest, very often.

The risks of exposing children to electronic devices at an early age

Here is a brief example that illustrates what seems to me to be the most serious aspect of the early use of electronic devices.

On a train trip to Madrid, some parents with their 3-year-old son sat behind me. In the seat in front of me were some younger parents with their 9-month-old daughter. The little girl was at the age where she could stand up, look around, and persuade others to smile at her when she gave her friendly smiles to those of us nearby. On the other hand, the 3-year-old boy behind me kept talking to his father and asking him many questions. For example, *"Which is faster, a train or a motor-cycle? Are those horses? etc."* He did not stop talking and occasion-ally asked his father for his cell phone: *"Dad, can I borrow your cell phone?"* The father calmly answered: *"No, not now."* On the contrary, when the 9-month-old girl got up, the mother sat down and gave her the tablet. The child would put it down and go back to looking at every-one, and the mother would sit her down. At one point, the child looked out the train window, and the mother put the tablet in front of her. On that occasion, the image of a woman appeared on the screen, and the girl touched it with her finger. At that moment, the father took her in his arms, and I thought she would finally have contact with the father without any electronics getting in the way. But when the father took his daughter in his arms, he held her in one arm while handling his cell phone with the other hand, paying more attention to it than his daughter.

I thought, *"What a difference!"* The little boy behind me was enjoying talking to his father, asking questions, commenting, being interested in the things of the world, and having fun with his father, who was accompanying him in this exciting life experience. On the other hand, the little girl was missing out on that experience and, in the worst-case scenario, not knowing that this experience existed. She experienced that the relationship with her parents brings a lot of sat-isfaction and security and that she is being lovingly cared for. That seminal experience was being lost for the little girl; the cell phone took its place.

I then questioned whether, in the face of the difficulties and hard-ships of life, the child in the back would feel he could count on his parents, but the little girl probably would not. This emptiness will have serious consequences in the future because she may not even know that this possibility—that of having a strong bond with her parents—exists. And what has not been experienced or experienced enough will not be able to awaken the desire to seek it. What I want to emphasize is that they will not even be able to be aware of what they are missing. That implies the experience of not being loved unconditionally or loved for being themselves. They will not feel they are getting *"likes"* from their parents. Over time, they will look for *"those likes"* that did not arrive through their mobile phones. That is why it is so important to play, talk, share experiences, etc. with children. If they reach adolescence full of *"likes"* from their parents, they will feel more confident about themselves and will not desperately look for those likes on social networks.

Sports, music, theater, and art: A good safeguard

I don't think it's a coincidence that it occurred to me to talk about this topic after discussing cell phones. I may have been induced to do so by the idea that if kids approach these activities, they can more easily *"contrast"* the significant difference between real and virtual satisfaction, obviously in favor of the real ones. Many fantasies, such as becoming famous YouTubers or influencers, can be dispelled more easily. Or at least introduce the idea that not everything in life is being a famous YouTuber or influencer; other things are also worthwhile. Let's not lose sight of the fact that we can all be seduced by the idea that grandiosity and popularity will make us rich and happy.

In general, I observe that sports, theater, or music are not given the role they deserve as regulators of the emotional development of children and adolescents. For example, playing sports (or just playing) is, in my opinion, a *"scaled-down"* representation of life's challenges. It requires effort, provides great satisfaction, disappointments and frustrating defeats, facilitates the assumption of one's limitations, the discovery of potential, promotes respect for the opponent, the acceptance of rules or rules of the game, the management of rivalry, the containment of anger, the acceptance of the authority and decisions of the coaches, the enhancement of physical conditions, teamwork, the idea of the need for improvement, and the setting of goals.

All these issues, which are decisive for growing up, unfold in sports activities. Hence, I believe playing sports, arts, playing, and playing theater is a priority in children's education. It is one of the best vaccines against the risk of a possible relationship with addictions or the establishment of a personality structure tending towards addiction insofar as the management of frustration is inherent to the practice of sport, as it is in life. Activities easily become part of family conversations and provide endearing and create many unforgettable family moments.

However, parents should be cautious about this in one aspect. It is not uncommon for them to generate high expectations about their children's sporting future, to want their son or daughter to be a future sports star, and to demand too much of them. This is risky because it can translate into enormous pressure on their children that, paradoxically, can end up increasing frustration since becoming an elite athlete is a complex path that depends on many other factors, including chance or coincidence. The *"rising star"* can fall into severe depression when, for any reason, such as an injury, their predicted and glorious expectations are cut short. If we really have a child gifted in sports, art, etc. The best thing to do is not to rush into it, to remind them that their studies are still necessary, and not to *"get too excited."* Sometimes, the parents' desire is so great that they end up in fights with the referees, with the parents of the children of the other team, even coming to blows. The children who watch these *"spectacles"* suffer enormously because of the shame their parents cause them, and they feel very guilty.

We all know cases of famous athletes, artists, etc., who fall into deep depressions that lead to addictions when their professional careers end, and they find themselves with an unbearable emptiness.

With this risk in mind, I believe that sports should be one of the central protagonists in children's lives. If I had the power, I would recommend that they practice sports daily in schools and hold competitions.

Both music and theater and other artistic endeavors allow developments similar to those of sports: teamwork, the development of verbal and corporal communication as a way of expressing emotions, neutralizing shyness, etc. I won't go any further because I understand that the advantages are apparent, just as in sports. However, it is essential that all these activities be understood as a game, not as an obligation in the children's daily lives, and above all, that they enjoy them. Not everyone has to do sports or theater, but whatever they like best. This means that, sometimes, parents have to *"try"* different activities until they find the one that best suits their children's interests.

I don't think it is very advisable to flood children with activities. They often have *"workdays"* longer than those of their parents or teachers, something that I think should be detected by common sense. And if parents can promote curiosity in their children and generate real challenges, it will help protect them from the fantasy that happiness will come from fame.

Last comment

Many parents, despite my explanations, tell me: *"Ok, but what do we do?"* My answer is that it is advisable to limit the mobile, not abruptly, and explain the reasons as many times as necessary (which are usually many times). And be able to contemplate that, after excessive cell phone use, there may be an internal conflict that should be investigated because this excess is usually one *"symptom"* of an underlying problem (insecurity, shyness, intolerance of frustration, etc). A determining indicator that there is an underlying conflict is that your children cannot *"let go"* of it. In that case, it is advisable to ask for help.

Note

1   This happened with a group of teenagers talking about cell phones.

Reference list

Balint, M. (1963). On being empty of oneself. *The International Journal of Psychoanalysis*, 44:470.

Balint, M. (1968). *The basic fault*. London: Tavistock Publications.

Bertolini, R., and Nissim, S. (2002). Video games and children's imagination. *Journal of Child Psychotherapy*, 28(3):305–325.

Bion, W. R. (1959). Attacks on linking. *International Journal of Psychoanalysis*, 40:308–315.

Britton, R. (1998). *Belief and imagination. Explorations in psychoanalysis*. Routledge.

Ferenczi, S. (1926). *The problem of acceptance of unpleasant ideas in advances knowledge of the sense of reality*. Further Contributions, London: Karnack Books (1980).

Fonagy, P., and Target, M. (1996). Predictors of outcome in child psychoanalysis: A retrospective study of 763 cases at the Anna Freud Center. *Journal of the American Psychoanalytic Association*, 44:27–73.

Freud, S. (1904). The psychopathology of everyday life. In *The standard edition of the complete works of Sigmund Freud*, Vol. VI. London: Hogarth Press (1950–74).

Freud, S. (1911). Formulations on the two principles of mental functioning. In *The standard edition of the complete works of Sigmund Freud*, Vol. XII. London: Hogarth Press (1950–74).

Freud, S. (1920). *Más allá del principio del placee*. Obras Completas de Sigmund Freud, Vol. 18. Ed. Amorrortu.

Furman, E. (1999). The impact of parental interventions. *International Journal of Psychoanalysis*, 80:172.

Icart, A., and Freixas, J. (2020). *A mí no me pasa nada*. Octaedro.

Schoffer, D. (2008). *La Función Paterna en la Clínica Freudiana*. Lugar Editorial.

Steiner, J. (1997). *Refugios Psíquicos*. Biblioteca Nueva.

Sugarman, A. (2017). The transitional phenomena functions of smartphones for adolescents. *Psychoanalytic Study of the Child*, 70:135–150.

Winnicott, D. (1958). The capacity to be alone. *The International Journal of Psychoanalysis*, 39:416.

Winnicott, D. W. (1951). Transitional objects and transitional. In *Through pediatrics to psychoanalysis*. London: Hogarth Press (1987).

Chapter 13

Teaching patience
Building frustration tolerance

Cayetano García-Castrillón Armengou

The issue of desires and needs and managing frustration is complex in families, as it brings together the desires and needs of parents and children. Moreover, each family member manages both the delay in its achievement and the transitory or definitive frustration of a desire differently. In other words, each deals with it as they know how or as they can. Moreover, priorities differ. What may be a priority for a mother may not be so for her partner, which leads to a particular need for consensus with concessions and compromises. However, the children's priorities are usually quite different from those of the parents, as is logical.

The following simile would be helpful: the family has to go to a celebration, and the mother needs time to get ready, time that the children demand to help them get dressed. The eldest of the children complains because he is a teenager and *"can't be bothered by"* the family celebration, but he has to go. The father, in turn, scolds the son because he is delaying everyone, demanding the use of the bathroom, which the mother needs to comb the youngest daughter's hair, etc. They all experience and perceive the incident differently.

Clearly, the family, in these circumstances, can lose patience because they deal with the frustration in different ways: the teenager doesn't want to go, the father is frustrated at having to be on top of him, the mother runs out of time for herself and, on top of that, she gets a run in her stocking at the last minute, while the youngest daughter waits her turn. For any of them, things are not going as they would like. It is difficult to say what frustration is, at least in words, but in short, we could define it as an annoying feeling of varying intensity that emerges when what we want is not achieved, partially or entirely. This is where what I called earlier frustration management takes place and on which

DOI: 10.4324/9781003581543-15

the outcome will depend. In turn, management will depend on the capacity for what psychoanalysts call *"containment,"* which, simply put, is *"learning to wait."* (I clarify that when I speak of frustrations, I am not referring to traumatic moments in life. Those imply a complex emotional analysis).

At birth, the baby has many needs that should be met without delay due to his lack of autonomy and the importance of strengthening the bond with his parents. Thus, a breastfed baby feels supported, cared for, fulfilled, and loved. But if, for whatever reason, the breastfeeding is *"delayed,"* the baby despairs. We have all witnessed this when we hear a baby's cries take on intense and desperate overtones (which is why it is so common to see mothers lovingly telling their babies, *"Calm down, I'm here").* As the baby gets older, he learns to tolerate waiting. Thus, if he is hungry at age 5, you can tell him to wait for a while, and he will not cry inconsolably because he knows that, eventually, his hunger will be satisfied. That is to say, little by little, children learn that the satisfaction of their desire will come, even if they have to wait a while. Let's see two situations that can alter this process:

Two scenarios that challenge this process

a. If parents, by default, immediately satisfy all their child's desires, learning to manage waiting does not occur—and, logically, neither does learning to manage frustration. Something is missing when parents understand that giving their children the best and being excellent parents means showing them that they will not lack anything and that they will not even have to wait to receive what they want. This usually occurs when the parents themselves have lived a very deprived childhood. It is a kind of *"rebound effect,"* not wanting their child to go through even the slightest deprivation or delay—deprivations and delays that affect them so much. Deep down, they fear their children may feel the same way they did. This reaction inadvertently confuses many parents. However, the child understands it differently, which leads the child to believe that the parents or others will always provide what the child wants without delay. Thus, whenever he gets frustrated, he will blame the other person for not having *"supplied him with what he wanted,"* which he is used to. These children become tyrants and always believe they are owed something. This gives rise to a tyrannical management of frustration, the need for their desires to be satisfied immediately, and a tendency to become addicted to the understanding that *"one must never wait"* to satisfy their desires. If waiting occurs, they experience it as aggression from the other towards them and react violently. In fact, many of the aggressions by children against parents nowadays are produced by what I have described, although naturally, more factors are at play.

b. That parents do not understand that the process occurs gradually and hurry it. For example, if they have to go to nursery school and skip the adaptation period, the child may experience the wait or the farewell as horrible. Let us remember that children experience time at a slower pace than adults (we all remember the long summers as children and the short summers as adults). Another example is the widespread misunderstanding that holding a child too much is wrong because they *"can get used to it,"* which suggests that children will become attached to their parents. These misunderstandings scare many parents, and they delay holding their children. Believe me, it is not a terrible thing to hold a baby or a child as often as they ask for it; quite the contrary. Or the idea of *"let them wait, it's not time to breastfeed,"* etc. All this provokes a wait that can become unbearable and generate the experience that their desires (unlike in the previous case) will never be met or that they are not being paid attention to. In short, the child is unknowingly asked for more than they can give according to their development. In these situations, the children learn that they are taken into little consideration or not at all; their reasonable wishes are excluded and replaced by the wishes of the parents, who are moving fast. This results in children desperately seeking to satisfy their desires. This usually happens because parents understand that their children's early dependencies are the manifestation that their growth will be stalled. In other words, they experience dependency as a grave danger and act accordingly to defuse this threat, which leads them to understand that if they address their child, they will seriously harm them. It is crucial for parents to realize that early dependence is an essential phase in development because, thanks to it, the bond is greatly strengthened, along with their child's inner confidence and emotional security. When this security and inner confidence are sufficiently established, the child will undergo the search for independence without fear and with the feeling that the world is full of things to explore and experience. Children will surely tell their parents enthusiastically about their *"own discoveries in life."*

However, if these concerns and fears of early dependencies persist, when children are older, they may resort to lying. At older ages, this acceleration usually translates into an excess of parental control, from which the children will try to escape, as I said before. It is curious to observe how parents who have fallen into the trap of acceleration and control ask the child: *"You are not lying to me, are you?"* *Deep* down, they know that with so much pressure, children may not have any other way. In other words, before the action of control appears, the reaction of escape through the lie comes.

At other times, the child will try to be an absolute reflection of what his parents tell him, admitting and accepting parental control. I call this the *"cell tower syndrome,"* like the amplifier antennas for cell phones that send the same signal back and forth from one to another. The risk is that the situation will explode sooner or later because the child's inner security and confidence will be significantly weakened.

But usually, things go acceptably well, and it is the children who have to understand and recognize that, many times, desires will not be satisfied immediately and that they must wait.

How can children be taught to wait?

As you get older, it takes longer to achieve your desires; it takes more time to do it. All families transmit this in one way or another with phrases such as: *"You'll play later." "It's time to do homework now." "It can't be when you say."* Thus, for example, when they did not have to do homework, they could go to play beforehand, but as the school year progressed, this changed. Comments like these include the benefits of learning to wait, but the children tend to experience it as a prohibition. Let's not forget that they come from their baby stage, where every desire was attended to quickly, and now they experience the delay as something very annoying.

That's why I think you have to explain it, for example, *"then it can be," "then you can play,"* and so on. You may say, *"We already do that."* Well, that's particularly good because it helps a lot. But sometimes, we can fall a little short, and expanding on what we say may be necessary. For example:

Later, you may be able to do it, but now you have to take a bath, and for the record, I am not doing it to annoy you. It is necessary to take a bath. My child, I would like to have a snack now, but I have

*to wait, too. Later, when we can have a snack, we'll have an enjoy-
able time.*

This is just a brief insight. I'm sure your parents have your own
ideas along these lines. I encourage you to persevere. Children usually
understand this. Of course, every child is different and may expect
more and others less. Let's see a brief example. Parents once said,
"We have already told them that, and it doesn't work." After this comment, I said something about the importance of perseverance: *"Do you
do any sports?" "What sport?" "Paddle tennis." "With a coach?"
"Sure." "How many times did the coach make you repeat the same
thing in different ways until you got it right?" "A lot. We were very
clumsy at first."* I told them that kids need time, as well. They laughed
for a good while, and so did I. Afterwards, I explained that it is surprising how sometimes we believe that with children, there is a kind
of *"magical and immediate learning."* That doesn't exist in paddle
tennis or with children. I also explained to them that their desire to see
immediate results did not allow them to see the wisdom, in my opinion, of their course of action and their reconciliation with their child.
Frequently, impatience plays a trick on parents, and they think they are
not doing well when, in fact, their own creativity in the education of
their children is excellent.

In other words, waiting provides more satisfaction than frustration,
while immediacy is a considerable source of frustration, although it
may seem the opposite.

Reference list

Balint, M. (1952). Early developmental stages of the ego. In *Primary
love and psycho-analytic technique*. London: Hogarth Press (1973).

Balint, M. (1963). On being empty of oneself. *The International Journal of Psychoanalysis*, 44:470.

Bick, E. (1962). Symposium on child analysis: Child analysis today.
International Journal of Psychoanalysis, 43:328–332.

Freud, S. (1920). *Más allá del principio del placer*. Obras Completas
de Sigmund Freud, Vol. 18. Ed. Amorrortu.

Freud, S. (1927). The future of an illusion. In *The standard edition of
the complete works of Sigmund Freud*, Vol. XXI. London: Hogarth
Press (1950–74).

Furman, E. (1995). Working with and through the parents. *Child Analysis: Clinical, Theoretical and Applied*, 6:21–42.

Isaacs, S. (1952). The nature and function of phantasy. In M. Klein, P. Heimann, S. Isaacs and J. Riviere (eds.), *Developments in psycho-analysis*. London: Hogarth Press (1970).

Kashdan, T. B., McKnight, P. E., Fincham, F. D., and Rose, P. (2011). When curiosity breeds intimacy: Taking advantage of intimacy opportunities and transforming boring conversations. *Journal of Personality*, 79(6):1067–1099.

Malberg, N. T. (2015). Activating mentalization in parents: An integrative framework. *Journal of Infant, Child & Adolescent Psychotherapy*, 14:232–245.

Schoffer, D. (2008). *La Función Paterna en la Clínica Freudiana*. Lugar Editorial.

Segal, H. (1982). *Introduccion a la obra de Melanie Klein*. Paidos.

Segal, H. (1994). Phantasy and reality. *The International Journal of Psychoanalysis*, 75(2):395–401.

Wechsler, E. (2011). La transmisión del Psicoanálisis. Teoría de la técnica de las entrevistas preliminares y de la supervisión. *Revista de Psicoanálisis (APM. Asociación Psicoanalítica de Madrid)*, 63:158–170.

Wechsler, E. (2013). *Herencias: la transmisión en psicoanálisis*. Ed. Letra Viva.

Winnicott, D. (1953). Transitional objects and transitional phenomena- A study of the first not-me possession. *The International Journal of Psychoanalysis*, 34:89.

Winnicott, D. W. (1960). The theory of the parent-infant relationship. In *The maturational processes and facilitating environment*. London: Hogarth Press (1965).

Chapter 14

Grandparents

Their crucial place in the modern family

Cayetano García-Castrillón Armengou

I find it striking how little importance is given in psychiatry, psychology, and psychoanalysis to the role of grandparents in family life. However, they provide crucial emotional support for parents and grandchildren daily. The support ranges from logistical help to a tension-stabilizing function. Picking up the grandchildren from school, caring for them if they are ill, passing on their experiences, providing the grandchildren with an illustration of love, affection, and tenderness free from the demands of daily upbringing, passing on family history, and, in many cases, being exceptional and amusing confidants, are some of the invaluable contributions of grandparents. Grandparents rarely play a disruptive role in family life.

That doesn't mean that relationships are not strained at times, especially for first-time parents and grandparents. When their children have their babies, their grandparents begin. This transition unconsciously reminds them of their distant experiences of paternity and maternity, which they experience as a kind of mourning. Some grandparents react by trying to play the role of parent again, which often strains relationships. Typically, there is a period of adaptation to the change (as always) until each one is resituated in their new role. The situation tends to normalize if the new grandparents and the new parents do not take it as a confrontation or rejection.

Once this common pitfall is overcome, the role of grandparents takes on a much broader and enriching dimension. Let us take a brief example: Lucia was entering her adolescence and regularly ate with Lola, her maternal grandmother, who served Lucia whatever she felt like eating, especially a Spanish omelet with onions. A privilege that Lucia does not enjoy at her parents' house because Grandmother Lola's Spanish omelet with onions is *"unbeatable."* While Lucia, rebellious

DOI: 10.4324/9781003581543-16

as befitted her age, did not tell her mother anything, she openly told her grandmother everything. Lucia's mother was surprised at the degree of trust she had with her grandmother but not with her. This made Lucia's mother somewhat angry, but at the same time, she was grateful, *"at least there is someone who knows what is happening with her,"* she often commented.

She (Lucia) also commented, *"My mother didn't make me Spanish omelets every time I asked her to, only sometimes."* But grandma does for her. The grandmother listened to all her granddaughter's trials and tribulations and laughed while telling her about her own when she was young, encouraging Lucia to take the plunge. Usually, Lucia would tell her grandmother, *"Don't tell my mother about this,"* although she didn't make her promise. Somehow, Lucia knew that information from her teenage life would reach her mother sooner or later. Grandmother tended, wisely, to de-dramatize the clashes between Lucia and her mother. That is, the grandmother did not ally herself with Lucia's adolescent rebelliousness, and she showed her more serene, adult, and sensible reference to things and her mother.

In a way, she contained a lot of her granddaughter's impulses. At her grandmother's, Lucia would clear the table, wash the dishes, help in the kitchen, etc. While at home, she didn't do that at all; it was *"too humiliating to obey her mother like a little girl."* When the mother heard this, she was surprised and wondered why Lucia did this with her grandmother and not with her. Logically, with a certain amount of anger. She also said that it seemed that she had two different daughters. The mother mentioned that it was good that the grandmother did not engage in her daughter's criticisms towards her. As time went by, I had the opportunity to ask Lucia why she spent so much time with her grandmother, to which she responded that she was a teenager and wanted to get out of the house.

This example shows how, many times, children find in their grandparents a path of communication and support in matters that, in principle, they do not encounter or dare to seek with their parents because they fear too intense a clash and prefer to *"leave the house"* to avoid greater evils; basically, to protect the relationship with their parents, as Lucia told me (when I could talk with her, as I said before). Lucia's grandmother gave her this opportunity (to talk) without undermining her daughter (Lucia's mother). This function of listening to dialogue and tolerance eventually paved the way for dialogue between Lucia and her mother.

At first, when the three of them, grandmother, mother, and granddaughter, got together, the mother tended to scold Lucia, *"You tell grandmother, but not me."* The grandmother very tactfully replied, *"It's because I laugh and am amused by what she tells me."* In my opinion, this grandmother is great for the following reasons: she does not criticize her daughter and explains to her that she is in a more comfortable position and has a better outlook on life than she does. She takes the drama out of the situation. The mother immediately understood and responded to that, of course, because she was the mother. In addition, the grandmother, as I commented before, never disqualified her daughter, Lucia's mother, respected her as a mother (she did not rival her), and respected her granddaughter Lucia's rebelliousness. Over time, Lucia's grandmother's attitude allowed for marvelous three-way communication.

Another example is that of Grandfather Anthony, a passionate soccer lover. As soon as his first grandson was born, he made him a member of his team's fan club, and as soon as he could take him to the games, he did so. When his grandson became a teenager, he continued the *"tradition of going with his grandfather to soccer,"* an unbreakable tradition for both. However, as his grandfather told me, his grandson wore piercings and super modern clothes while his style was more *"classic."* The aesthetic contrast amused the grandfather. Both talked about the divine and the human in these *"encounters."* These experiences with grandparents are priceless. It was common for Anthony to ask his grandfather how he did it with his father: *"Grandfather, did you let him dress the way he wanted? What curfew did you put him on?"* Anthony often told his grandfather that his father was stricter with him, and his grandfather told him to give him time. On other occasions, he asked his grandfather to intercede for him with his father. Grandfather would do so with a lot of tact towards his son, which resulted in Anthony's improved relationship with his father.

That is to say, beyond the permissiveness that grandparents provide, there is the role of a repository of the grandchildren's confidence and secrets that indirectly smooths tensions with the parents. If we pay attention, many grandchildren seek to talk to their grandparents about things. Moreover, this happens regardless of age. I think some parents don't understand this and decide to *"dictate"* to the grandparents what they can and can't say or determine what they can and can't do with the grandchildren. Let's look at an example. During the summer, grandparents Thomas and Mary invited their six grandchildren to their country house with a swimming pool and amenities that all their grandchildren clearly appreciated. During their stay, Grandma took wonderful care of them all. However, given Mary's age, she became very tired and needed help. This led her to ask for more cooperation from her grandchildren, which was not forthcoming, so Grandma became angry with them. Mary was conflicted about the attitude to take. Her first option was to consider that she does everything better and that if she insisted on her grandchildren's help, she would end up with more work. Evidently, when Mary told me this, I noticed that this justification did not convince her either. This prompted me to ask her if there was any reason why she was afraid to call the grandchildren to order. Her answer was clear and concise, *"My daughter-in-law told me that I could not scold her children because the children's upbringing was up to her and her husband (Mary's son)."* She was afraid that her daughter-in-law would get angry and not allow them to go to the country house anymore. After this explanation, she told me that her nine-year-old grandson, the youngest of all, said to her, *"Grandma, I'll help you. You are doing a lot."* She was very grateful for this offer. However, it never ceased to amaze her that the *"older"* grandchildren did not realize how overworked she was. Mary felt trapped.

In discussing this situation, Thomas, Mary, and I theorized that her daughter-in-law might be concerned that if Mary exercised her authority as a grandmother in her house to ask for cooperation and help, it would be a disavowal of her daughter-in-law's authority or that the grandmother wanted to *"take her place."* We thought it might be good to talk it over with the daughter-in-law to lessen the resentment and anger that this situation was generating in the grandparents, especially Mary. It might also help to explain to the daughter-in-law that if the grandparents did not correct the grandchildren, they would end up understanding that the grandparents only exist to be at their service, thus making it difficult for them to learn that the grandparents must also be taken care of, as they have done so many times with them. Finally, everything became clear. In similar situations, it is common for parents, fearful of being overruled by the grandparents, to have a child (usually the oldest) exercise parental authority in the absence of the parents. I call this the *"ambassador child syndrome,"* which is the one in charge of tasks in the absence of the parents. It is a difficult, although attractive position, for the *"chosen one."* He feels the rivalry with his siblings disappears because he is now in charge. This shows many suspicions and resentments among the siblings, among many other things.

However, to me, this is an unnecessary attitude (on the part of the parents). The freedom that parents give grandparents will always be an excellent avenue for communication and a loving relationship. Obviously, if the grandparents have failed to understand their role and are trying to substitute for the parents, it is logical for the parents to put limits on the grandparents. Still, the most practical thing is to ask grandparents not to *"interfere by playing second parents"* because of the risks involved. However, they are usually not very interested in this. Many say, *"I've had my turn to be a parent, and I've had enough."*

As I pointed out earlier, these possible interferences are more common with the first grandchildren when everyone is new in their role (parents and grandparents). Grandmothers, especially, may experience this as an extra responsibility, to the extent that they experience this situation as a vulnerable moment for their daughter: *"Now I have to go back to taking care of my daughter and grandchild."* As I explained at the beginning of the book, this concern can provoke an action-reaction situation. In other words, this worry can send grandmothers into *"hyper-action"* mode, but they are usually incredibly helpful, which doesn't hurt anything. This usually dissipates when things calm down, and the grandmothers see that the mother and baby are settled. The new mothers end up finding rest, protection, and essential and comforting security in their grandmother. In fact, after childbirth, the presence of the grandmother is usually a huge relief for moms and also for dads. Grandmothers have experience; they know how to handle the baby. They have been through the same thing, and that contribution is very reassuring. It also allows moms to rest after childbirth, which is also very important. Thanks to the progressive assessment of the maternal aspects in the parents and the significant contribution that it implies, the idea that the initial upbringing falls exclusively on the mother is being left behind. Grandparents (and fathers) also perform maternal functions.

Here is an example of the influence that grandparents can have on the lives of their grandchildren. Peter is the eldest of several siblings. For various reasons, when he was very young, Peter's parents decided that he had to move far away from the rest of his family. He went from living in the countryside to living in a cold, concrete city far from his home, town, landscapes, animals, parents, and siblings. Logically, this affected him greatly, and he felt enormous nostalgia for everything left behind. Moreover, returning would be impossible in the short and medium term. Any request to return was rejected, to the point of having to give up the idea that one day he would return.

Peter commented that one day during a visit, one of his grandfathers gave him a sheep and that, on another occasion, his other grandfather gave him a box with two white doves; and that the same grandfather, when he insisted on wanting a small flock of sheep, asked some *"gentlemen"* if it was possible to get those sheep. Peter remembers how happy he was as a child to see that his grandfather had asked and had taken his wish seriously. Even so, he had to return to the sad, dark city. Finally, as an adult, he could have his own small livestock farm, which he tended and cared for with passion. We could see how vital Peter's grandfathers were to him in that they made him feel that all was not lost and that they accepted his wishes, which, in a way, allowed Peter never to give them up. This emotional inheritance was invaluable for him, as it is for so many other grandchildren.

I think it is essential for parents not to be afraid to tell grandparents what is bothering them so that they can readjust. This is much better than brooding in silence or complaining to the partner about how badly the grandparents are doing.

On the other hand, one of the most widespread misunderstandings among parents is the belief that the intervention of grandparents can dismantle what they have built concerning their children's education since the rules governing the relationship of grandparents with grandchildren do not coincide with those of parents with their children. This can cause parents to become defensive in trying to match the grandparents' standards with their own. As I pointed out earlier, they do this by constantly telling the grandparents what they can and cannot do, say or not say, etc. In the worst cases, this can end in two ways: one, by limiting the grandchildren's encounters with the grandparents, and the other, by cutting off the relationship altogether. This is very depressing for grandparents and can generate a lot of pain for grandchildren.

Parents frightened by these discrepancies do not realize that their children can tell the difference between the rules with mom and dad and with their grandparents, just as the rules at school also differ from those at home. Many of these fears disappear if parents understand their children's ability to differentiate. Special mention should be made of the fact that there are disputes during the separation process where grandparents are used as a weapon. If this happens, there is nothing more painful for grandparents and grandchildren.

Another common situation is that the grandparents are too *"lonely"* because the grandchildren rarely visit them or are reluctant to do so. I think it is essential for parents to explain to their children that feelings of loneliness are very distressing and that they should keep this aspect in mind so as not to make the grandparents suffer unnecessarily. In general, the children understand immediately.

But often, grandparents are no longer around, and I think it is important for parents to talk about them, to tell their children what they were like so that their children can remember them, even if their absence is painful. If it is still possible to enjoy time with them, the life experience they transmit, their ability to dialogue, to de-dramatize, to compensate, to soothe, to serve as a bridge of communication, of moderation, are invaluable experiences for the grandchildren. Even better, it enhances the relationship with the grandparents. Needless to say, in working with families, whether with parents or children, the presence of a good relationship with grandparents is a favorable indicator in all senses.

In addition, the number of single-parent families is increasing, and one of the grandparents often performs essential parental functions.

One last point, honestly, this chapter is a tribute to grandparents.

Part III

Psychoanalysis and parenting

Chapter 15

A fruitless endeavor

The development of the emotional vaccine[1]

Cayetano García-Castrillón Armengou

When faced with any difficulty that worries them, and before consider-ing asking for professional help, parents will try to fix the problem. In truth, they make a diagnosis of the issue under a significant level of anxiety, as is logical. If, despite their attempts, things still don't work out, they become increasingly more worried. It is at that point that they usually seek help. We see how these parents explain their discourage-ment and that they have already tried *"everything."* In the case that follows, we can also observe the parents' experience and efforts before going to the professional.

Parents' efforts before seeking professional help

Let's look at an example of work with parents who are very worried about their 13-year-old daughter, who studies hard, but the academic results achieved do not match the effort and the hours she spends stud-ying. The parents thought that all the work was *"in vain"* and that this was increasingly discouraging to her. They were becoming seriously concerned about this situation, which seemed to have no end and no viable way out: *"Her grades do not reflect the amount she studies."* After consulting different entities, including the attention deficit hyper-activity disorder diagnosis, it looked increasingly like a hodgepodge; we began to think about the situation.

They told me that the siblings were brilliant in their studies and that they had tried everything with her: private teachers, restricting her time on the cell phone, rewards, punishments, meetings with teachers, etc. In other words, the parents were looking for solutions to alleviate their

DOI: 10.4324/9781003581543-18

concerns and their daughter's suffering, which, as I said before, were sinking little by little. The parents feared that if things did not change (and with superb judgment, in my opinion), she would *"throw in the towel"* and stop studying. That sad ending seemed very possible to me.

Otherwise, they showed great regard for their daughter and considered her honorable and kind-hearted. I also considered that the parents, being accustomed to the excellent academic careers of the older children, were puzzled when they received grades different from what they were used to seeing. After this first contact with the parents, I spoke with their daughter.

She tells me that she is the youngest of several siblings who are extraordinarily brilliant in academics but that *"things don't work out for her no matter how hard she tries."* From the beginning, she is willing to talk, fed up with the situation. On the other hand, it seemed to me that she felt inferior to others, insecure and discouraged, as her parents were. She also relayed that she'd previously suffered episodes of bullying that were resolved well, thanks to the school's collaboration. She tells me that she gets distracted easily and spends many hours studying or *"pretending to study"* when she no longer understands anything. Also, when her parents realize she's distracted, tensions arise, followed by reprimands, and she feels terrible because she doesn't know how to avoid it. She says, *"I can't help it. I'm constantly going to do something else." "My brothers and sisters can help it."* This girl clearly felt inferior compared to her siblings.

However, when talking to her, she seemed intelligent, approachable, and eager to grow but very discouraged regarding her academic possibilities, lamenting that there was no way to improve her grades, and focused on what we were discussing, which resoundingly ruled out ADHD.

Everyone was worried about the future outlook. This led to a distressing situation dominated by repeated attempts to get the academics under control, private tutors, meetings with teachers, and reprimands that the cell phone was the focus of the problem. That is, a suffocating environment where there seemed to be nothing good. This spiral grew and grew. Thus, for everyone, each exam became life-defining, of her future, of whether she would succeed or if everything had gone irremediably wrong.

Entering an exam with this heavy backpack caused her to freeze. Studying became a nightmare. Obviously, she was distracted by the cell phone and also without the phone. Her self-image was deteriorating rapidly. When collaborating with parents, I tried to show them these aspects, which had led to an -involuntary- lack of recognition motivated by the stress that also invaded them. At the same time, it seemed to me that their daughter was a person with enormous potential. I could have a more unrestricted view of the anxiety than the parents. So, we planned a change of strategy in the relationship with their daughter. Essentially, we planned to applaud anything that she did well. That was my proposal because I understood that she had forgotten that things could sometimes work out for her since she also felt trapped. I tried to explain this to the parents so they would understand that I believed this new way of approaching their daughter made sense. I pointed out to them that, naturally, I did not own the magic pill and that if they agreed to try, we could have a chance to see what happened, whether it could work or not. And then we'd keep observing.

From my point of view, it is imperative to make it truly clear that neither I nor the parents have absolute certainty of what can work or not, and we will have to assume that uncertainty is natural and inevitable. And that I, as a professional, as well as them in their parental roles, are subject to renouncing the dangerous temptation of *"expecting things to be solved in one stroke."* We'd all like the result. But the reality is hugely different.

However, by thinking, reflecting, opening new channels of communication, reviewing our experiences, backgrounds, etc., we can launch a task of trial and error-review-reflection, both for what does not work and what does (knowing what works and why it is also essential). It is that search that will help us, but it is important to remember that when anxiety invades us, haste makes its appearance systematically. But it doesn't help.

In my experience, it is common to observe that parents are somewhat perplexed when I say that I do not know what will immediately solve things, and often, that causes them to accept the proposals with a reasonable degree of skepticism. This is fine with me, so they know they can have the freedom to question me, to make them understand that I do not infantilize them and that this is a team effort. So, if things don't work out, they can also think about why they haven't worked out. Somehow, I try to make it easier for them to observe what is happening so that they can have more perspective on the situation. Increasing the ability to observe a child is a decisive initial objective because anxiety, haste, and discouragement nullify it.

Returning to the case I mentioned, it happened that, after about five months of work in which they systematically celebrated their daughter's achievements, the mother told me that, although her grades had not risen much, her mood had improved and that she made very colorful outlines, *"typical of the girls who do well."* That got the mother's attention. Meanwhile, the father told me that he worried she was getting too distracted by the cell phone, which could become a severe problem. In a clear desire to enhance the slight improvement she was showing, the father thought it would be good to restrict her cell phone use. I perceived, as I let the parents know, that maybe their daughter was more focused on studies because she felt more capable and that the fact that she made more colorful outlines indicated that she paid more attention to doing them (she thought that for her it was not all that gray anymore).

I presented them with the contradiction: *did the cell phone distract her, or did the burden of seeing everything as very gray?* I understood that it was the stress and that the cell phone was her distraction and a sedative in the face of the gloomy panorama she and her parents saw. I realized that the father had observed an *"excess of cell phone use"* at a time when it really functioned as a sedative. I added that if he, myself, or anyone else is overwhelmed, they will tend to be distracted by the cell phone or a fly passing in front of them. So, for that reason, I thought that the problem wasn't the phone and that, in fact, she was showing more focus through her colorful outlines.

Obviously, I told them that a cell phone, like other things, requires reasonable time management. The father's response was surprisingly good. He told me that he had let his daughter hang out with friends longer despite fearing that she would become more distracted. In short, it was a little scary for him. On another level, I saw that, for the father, reducing control over her frightened him, but he was willing to try, which was quite an accomplishment for him.

The conversation between father and daughter, in which the father showed his fear but at the same time understood that she wanted to be with her friends and have *"her adventures,"* seemed vital to me. And so, I told him:

> *Notice how your daughter will have received that you, her father, understand that you have different stances but that you respect her and trust that she will be able to manage. You are conveying to her that you are confident that her future will not be gray if she is guided by her own ideas and your difference to it.*

I added that for his daughter, who was so *"low,"* seeing that bargain was going to translate into a high. What is certain is that the one who got *"the high"* was me, seeing the father being able to speak to his daughter and the mother with that incredible ability to observe and assess her evolution. For me, at that moment, these determined parents broke out of the initial vicious circle of anxiety, fear, and worry that immobilized them and propelled them towards control, excessive restrictions, reproaches, depression, and discouragement. This is usually the beginning of the end of the conflict.

Note

1 Throughout the book, you will observe different references to teachers given their importance in the life of any child or adolescent and for their usual cooperation and support in the counseling processes. These sections have been prepared and reviewed in collaboration with Professor Blanca García-Castrillón Fernández.

Reference list

Piovano, B. (2004). Parenthood and parental functions as a result of the experience of parallel psychotherapy with children and parents. *International Forum of Psychoanalysis*, 13:187–200.

Slade, A. (2005). Parental reflective functioning: An introduction. *Attachment & Human Development*, 7:269–281.

Torras, E. (2012). *Normalidad, psicopatología y tratamientos en niños, adolescentes y familias*. Barcelona: Ed. Octaedro.

Wachs, C., and Jacobs, L. (2006). Introduction. In *Parent-focused child therapy: Attachment, identification, and reflective functions*. Ed. Jason Aronson. Inc.

Weisse, E. (1960). *The structure and dynamics of the human mind*. New York: Grune & Stratton.

Chapter 16

Family legacies

What we pass on

Cayetano García-Castrillón Armengou

In working with parents, I have detected their need to be listened to and supported. Sometimes, they say, *"It benefits us even more than our child."* They are often surprised once they clearly understand that they do many things to support the progress of their children's development. On other occasions, they are surprised to find that, without knowing it, they themselves may play a role in the conflicts that have arisen with their children. Now, I will present an example where a mother, worried about the constant confrontations with her adolescent son, discovers the transmission of what she received from her parents and how, by using them as a reference, the *"patterns"* are repeated.

In the periodic interviews that I conducted with the parents[1] every three weeks, the mother came without the father, who, when he came, was quite passive, leaving the reins of the interview to the mother.

Mother: *I feel so guilty. I did everything wrong. And I know that you are going to tell me that I am screwing up all the time. I feel terrible. But well, I have to tell you. That is how I feel.*

Analyst: *Well, you may feel very guilty, but then what? Do you punish yourself? It would not get us anywhere.*

Analyst: *Notice that you see me as someone who will only fixate on the negative, or that is what you consider wrong; I will, too.*

Mother: *Have I told you what my father is like? He didn't let us go out, always controlling; I had to be the good one,* the one who couldn't *fail in anything, the perfect one.*

Analyst: *I can see that you expected me to react similarly. It must have been so common that you also expected it from me. Didn't you?*

DOI: 10.4324/9781003581543-19

Mother: *Yes, (smile). My husband criticizes me for being too on top*
            of my son. He often talks back to me, and I get upset, but my
            husband does not intervene. He tells me that I nag my son
            (a clear identification with her father's behavior that she her-
            self criticized).

Mother: *But I am a bit overbearing, like my father. The truth is that*
            since I have been coming here, I try to stop myself, but some-
            times I can't, and I get angry when my husband doesn't help
            me or doesn't do what I say. My son suffered severe bullying.
            He fell apart. Since then, he has not been the same, and the
            worst thing is that it was his best friend who insulted and
            belittled him . . .

If we look at the sequence after the interpretation, she could see herself with more compassion, understand that her son is dealing with
the things that have happened to him, and not see him so much as
someone who complicates her life by not obeying her, as she did with
her father. She followed the same criteria as her father, which was
more or less: *"Daughter, you complicate everything if you don't obey*
me. Period."

This brilliant reflection by the mother allowed us to consider the
likelihood that changing to a more personal style could result in a better relationship with her son. When she was angry with her father, she
did not dare to tell him for fear of the consequences. If I had simply
told this mother from the beginning that she was too controlling and
that she should stop without asking her what she thought of her desire
to control, I would have conveyed to her that I only expected her to
obey me, like her father.

This approach would not have allowed her to reflect that she was
behaving like her father, expecting the child to obey only. After all, for
her father, the good daughter simply obeyed. Here lies the difference
between merely obeying me or understanding that she can manage the
search for her own style, one different from her father's, and bring
about change. (After this, she could detect that she was leaving little
space for her husband. It was clear that leaving space for the other
person was a threat).

It was evident that her 15-year-old son was rebelling against this situation. It was clear to me that her son was seeking his space like a typical teenager. Interestingly, the rebellion that his mother could not have
against her father. This gave me a lot to think about until one day when

I understood that the mother somehow showed her son that she would allow the rebellion. She must have conveyed to him that she would not be unyielding towards him for it. Months later, at a meeting with her son, he told me he was getting along better with his parents. At the end of the meeting, the parents arrived, and we all talked for a moment. The mother began by scolding her son for something insignificant, and she said automatically, *"There I go again. I have to take it easy!"* (She realized that she was repeating and transmitting *"the usual behavior"*). We all smiled at that moment.

In the following vignette, you will see these parents and their son's efforts to move forward. I must admit that seeing how parents strive to raise their children is an admirable and thrilling part of my job.

Mother:[2]   *Hi. Can I borrow a pen? How was your summer? Mine was fine. I have seen things in my son that I consider giant steps and others not so much. He has asked for something unthinkable: tutoring sessions for the school year. He has started and is incredibly happy. In addition, he told me that he wants to be more careful with food and eat healthier. He didn't say that before. Maybe I'm wrong, although you are "the professional," but I think when he gets impulsive, his head gets foggy; he doesn't think and sees everything as dark. His reasoning gets clouded. I recognize that impulsiveness in me.*

Analyst: *What an accurate observation; through self-observation, you have been able to identify the same behavior in him.*

Mother: *In the impulse, one sees that everything will go wrong and gets disoriented. It's the same for him. Understanding myself helps me to understand him, not like my father.*

Analyst: *I can see that you are finding and creating your own relationship style with your son, which is quite different from what you had with your father.*

Mother: *I used to be controlling; I couldn't control my impulses. I would be sincerely sorry to be like my father was with me with my son. But it's hard for him to relate to those in his age group. However, we talked more this summer. With his sister, it's a little better.*

Father: *The summer has been different in many ways.*

Let me add something more about this situation because it is quite common. While it is true that the son rebelled, he did it in a very childish and provocative way. This behavior, in turn, made the mother feel that she was right in controlling him increasingly. On the other hand, the father remained on the sidelines. This *"frame-work"* upset everyone and, at the same time, made each of them feel that their position was the correct one. Thus, nothing would change, but each person was convinced of *"their truth and their reasons for continuing to act the same way."* The focus of working with the son was to make him see that his *"childish"* rebellion was due to fear of coming to terms with his growth. He was *"cutting off his nose to spite his face."*

Showing the mother that she *"took the bait"* when dealing with these provocations was another focus of attention. And finally, conveying to the father the importance of *"daring to execute"* his functions was also crucial. In other words, the whole family structure was affected. Also, one of the determining factors in the possibility of things changing is that each family member does not fall into the idea that they possess the absolute truth. This unhealthy expression of narcissism would complicate everything enormously because unhealthy pride will cause a person's capacity for self-criticism to disappear in favor of relentlessly criticizing and blaming others. Fortunately, the levels of *"pride and narcissism"* in this family were not worrisome. However, if either pride or confusion is significant, the situation can enter what I call *"acceleration spirals."* This is essentially a continuous action-reaction response in family relationships with no room for thought or reflection, so the possibility of realistic change is impossible despite observing that no change occurs.

Types of family transmissions

Discovering, realizing, and understanding that we transmit many things to our children gives us the opportunity to change the old transmission to a new one (as this mother explained). Elina Wechsler brilliantly puts forward this idea in her book about Transmissions in Psychoanalysis.[3] Beyond the fact that parents or children may need help, the book's objective is for parents to detect what they are transmitting, and with this, many changes will occur naturally. Pausing to think helps to achieve this. Please understand this book in that sense—as a break to be able to observe a little further.

From my point of view, the *"transmission from parents to children"* consists of two parts. On the one hand, what I call *"emotional inheritance"* and on the other, *"relational inheritance."*

In the *"emotional inheritance,"* the dominant feelings received from the parents are reproduced. For example, suppose a father or mother is usually close and affectionate with his or her child. In that case, it is possible that, later on, when the child becomes a parent, they will integrate those emotions into the relationship with their child. This is because these aspects, identified during the child's upbringing, are understood to be a natural part of the relationship.

In *"relational inheritance,"* the dominant form of relationship is established with children. For example, if scolding is the usual practice in the child's upbringing, it will be repeated later. As I said before, it will also be seen as an integral part of the functioning of the parent-child relationship. This is how our parents become our references when confronting parenthood.

This process is normal, but sometimes, the *"inherited and transmitted"* generates difficulties. Changing what has been received is not easy because, deep down, it is understood that the new or different is *"inappropriate"* for becoming good parents. Parents hesitate when these new additions occur concerning their children. Incidentally, this explains why we always, in the initial interviews, probe and ask what their childhood and relationship with their parents was like. The general belief is that we do it to look for *"a traumatic event"* that can be determinant in a person's life; while that is true, we also look for *"emotional and relational inheritances."* Let's look at an example of what I have just explained where, perhaps, all this can be seen more clearly.

I remember a father who told me he was thrilled and proud that an elite rugby team had selected his son, although he was the youngest and most inexperienced member of the team. One day, he went out to play with the first team in a friendly match—it was his big debut. After the game, they celebrated this first step in their son's sporting career. However, the father criticized himself for having overindulged in his displays of joy. He thought he was taking the spotlight away from his son and making it his own.

This father had had a childhood with very emotionally distant parents who had great difficulty expressing warm emotions to their children (emotional inheritance). In addition, his parents strongly tended to establish a relationship with him based on constant reproaches (relational inheritance). This made him understand that *"transmitting his happiness"* was a significant failure.[4] At other times, his fear of *"messing up"* had led him to silence his displays of pride and appreciation for his children. This game was the first time he broke that *"tradition."* It seems he understood that the right thing to do was to continue with the same approach as his parents. He believed he had made a serious mistake despite having broken the transmission. I think Freud would have interpreted this as displacing the father by not following his criteria and *"daring to be a different and distinctive father."* Daniel Schoffer[5] discusses these aspects in his book of the paternal role and the importance of its functions.

I told this father that he was also a protagonist and participant in his son's success to the extent that he encouraged him, took him to the games, and always supported him. Why not celebrate it? I added that he would have liked his parents to have done it with him (to have inherited that). Finally, I told him that what he had really done was not to let the criteria that his parents passed on to him continue to *"operate in him,"* and perhaps that made him feel a little guilty.[6] That is, by understanding and challenging these inherited aspects, he could pass on more of himself to his son. In addition, I asked him how he thought his son would have felt if he had not conveyed his pride and satisfaction for what he was achieving. He responded, *"I can imagine because I was sad when they [my parents] didn't say anything to me about anything at all."*[7]

Another aspect to highlight in the transmission to children is the ways that parents use to communicate with them. The following example illustrates this. Recently, a good friend of mine, Jose, shared the following anecdote. During halftime of a basketball game for promising young players, the father of one of the players addressed his son, telling him in a harsh tone, *"Less shooting and more defending."* My friend recalled that the son made a face of disappointment at the father's comment. Right afterward, the coach approached and told him serenely, *"You played well. We will have to train more shots at the basket."* After the game resumed, a person sitting next to the father, who probably knew him, said, *"If you talk to your son like that, he will still love you, but he will stop loving himself."* The fact is the method of communication is critical.

Final consideration

Transmitting emotions is neither negative, harmful, nor a sign of weakness or a loss of authority. Don't parents who, patiently, little by little, help their child to ride a bicycle deserve to feel happy for having made it easier for them to do so? Finally, openly celebrating everyone's achievements is highly recommended.

Notes

1 This procedure was established at the beginning of the treatment, with the consent of the child, to whom the benefit of parental attendance every three weeks was explained.
2 What I have shown occurs after several months of working with all of them and where I consider that the process is already underway. (Alternate: This conversation takes place after several months of working with the family and where I consider that the process is already underway.)
3 Wechsler, E. (2013). *Herencias: la transmisión en psicoanálisis [Inheritance: Transmission in psychoanalysis]*. Ed. Letra Viva.
4 A concept used in other areas but not at all in psychoanalysis is traceability. As seen in this example, the path defining the paternal function begins with the parents' criteria, which are transmitted from parents to children. Examining traceability is very enlightening because it sometimes allows us to find out where the problem started.
5 Schoffer, D. (2008). *La Función Paterna en la Clínica Freudiana [The paternal function in the Freudian clinic]*. Lugar Ed.
6 When parents change, they often experience it in a distressing way. My understanding is that, deep down, there is a challenge to their parents *"even if it is deferred."*
7 It is quite common for fathers to conclude that getting emotional and expressing it is more of a mother's thing.

Reference list

Bion, W. R. (1962). *Learning from experience*. Maresfield Reprints, London: Karnac Books (1984).

Freud, S. (1911). Formulations on the two principles of mental functioning. In *The standard edition of the complete works of Sigmund Freud,* Vol. XII. London: Hogarth Press (1950–74).

Furman, E. (1999). The impact of parental interventions. *International Journal of Psychoanalysis*, 80:172.

Matte-Blanco, H. (1988). *Thinking, feeding and being.* London: Routledge.

Pichon Rivière, A. A. (1957). la inclusión de los padres en el cuadro de la situación analítica y el manejo de esta situación a través de la interpretación. *Revista de Psicoanálisis (REVAPA)*, 14:137–146.

Piovano, B. (2004). Parenthood and parental functions as a result of the experience of parallel psychotherapy with children and parents. *International Forum of Psychoanalysis*, 13:187–200.

Sandler, J. (2002). Acerca de la comunicación del paciente al analista: no todo es identificación proyectiva. In *Libro anual de psicoanálisis XVI*. São Paulo-Brasil: Ed. Escuta Ltda.

Wechsler, E. (2011). La transmisión del Psicoanálisis. Teoría de la técnica de las entrevistas preliminares y de la supervisión. *Revista de Psicoanálisis (APM)*, 63:158–170.

Wechsler, E. (2013). *Herencias: la transmisión en psicoanálisis*. Ed. Letra Viva.

Weisse, E. (1960). *The structure and dynamics of the human mind*. New York: Grune & Stratton.

Chapter 17

Parents in therapy

First steps toward inclusion[1]

*Cayetano García-Castrillón Armengou
and Frank García-Castrillón Armengou*

Introduction to parental involvement in therapy

Two considerations induced me to write this chapter. The first is that it brings together many of the aspects of the previous chapters, such as the importance of listening, the search for the ideal child, the importance of what children talk about, their desire to be understood, and the role of the person who listens to everyone—intermediaries such as grandparents, teachers, pediatricians, therapists, etc.—and how their contributions can break vicious circles in parent-child relationships. The second reason is that, astonishingly, the case occurred over 100 years ago, during the months of March and April 1909. Also, we owe it to Freud, little Hans, and his parents.

Little Hans, 5 years old, began to have many fears of horses. It all began after the birth of his sister and after observing a horse accident in the street where one died. Concerned, the parents consulted Freud to see if he could help them. Hans was a very expressive child, and, as you will see, he felt very confident in talking to his father, and he accepted Freud's help very willingly. In addition, Hans shows a very common attitude in children which is his desire to know more, asking many things and turning to his parents for it. On the other hand, Hans' parents showed the common belief that children are not educated enough to receive clear answers to their questions. Another frequent aspect that appears, as I have commented in previous chapters, is the expectation of having an ideal child. Surprisingly, Hans stands up for this.

Over the years, other psychoanalysts have continued to emphasize the importance of collaboration and assistance to parents. An important

DOI: 10.4324/9781003581543-20

part of mental health is integration. The parents aid their children's integration process despite difficulties. Parents and babies find a way to resolve basic conflicts, which enables them to experience joy and gratitude for having achieved it. These are memorable experiences for everyone. Also, Dr. Donald Winnicott (pediatrician and psychoanalyst) introduced the concept of the *"good enough mother"* in a clear reference to how it is not feasible to be a *"perfect"* mother or father and how this helps the formation of the baby's personality (the *self*) based on the parent's ability to adapt to the baby. He also introduced the concept of the *"facilitating environment,"*[2] which there is no need to explain because nowadays nobody questions it. Hence, the importance of helping parents.

The *"little Hans"* case: Lessons from psychoanalysis

I consider the *"case of little Hans"* as the first reported that includes parents. Little Hans's father had regular correspondence with Freud, in which he consulted him about his son's phobias (basically to horses), after which Freud answered him. Let us look at what Freud collected in his day concerning little Hans, a 5-year-old boy.

First vignette. Conversation with the son on March 13 sent to Freud by the father:

Father: *If you don't run your hand over your pee-pee anymore, the nonsense[3] will go away.*

Little Hans: *I don't run my hand over my pee-pee anymore.*

Father: *But you still want to do it.*

Little Hans: *But "wanting to" is not "doing," and "doing" is not "wanting to do."*

In a footnote, Freud says, *"Bravo, little Hans, I would not wish for adults a better understanding of psychoanalysis!"*

After this conversation, little Hans's fears diminished, but a few days later they were triggered again and seemed generalized: fear of giraffes, elephants, etc. In my opinion, what happened was that the father scolded him, saying that the mere fact of having the desire was bad enough. We could consider that the father did not provide a *"facilitating environment"* but rather an *"accusatory environment."*

Second vignette: The father and little Hans talk about his little sister. The father told little Hans that he would like his sister to die in the bathroom so that he could be left alone with *"Mom."* The father reproaches him, saying that a good child does not want that. After these comments, the following dialogue takes place between them:

Little Hans: But he has the right to think about it.
Father: But that's not right.
Little Hans: But if he thinks it, it's good. Write to the professor.
Father: You know. When Ana is older and can talk, you will love her more.
Little Hans: I already love her.

Obviously, it is clear that little Hans, despite his jealousy, loves his little sister. But the father insists this is wrong *("a good boy does not want that").* In other words, he is looking for the *"ideal child"* in his son, who should neither be jealous nor feel jealousy.

Afterward, little Hans asks him how the baby sister arrived (little Hans is curious). The father does not clarify it and continues to tell him that the stork brings babies. The father did not acknowledge his curiosity (nor did he facilitate it). Despite this answer, little Hans insisted on wanting to know more. It seems that little Hans was persistent in his curiosity because he was unsatisfied with the answer and insisted. Freud stressed to the father how important it was to clarify his son's questions. Freud began to detect the importance of children's curiosity and the advisability for parents not to avoid the frequent and customarily compromising questions from children with evasive answers (remember that this happened in March 1909, when nobody was talking about approaching children this way).

The father understood the importance of answering his son's questions, and after little Hans's repeated attempts to understand, clarification came from the father and mother. Finally, on April 24, the father writes to Freud, saying,

> *My wife and I enlightened little Hans; we told him that the children grow in mommy and then are brought into the world through pressure like the lump, which brings great pain . . . . In the afternoon, a great relief comes over him.*

Freud comments in this regard that *"the sexual curiosity of our Little Hans does not admit any doubt; it turns him into an investigator."*

Freud says that the appetite for knowledge and sexual curiosity seem inseparable from one another. The sexuality of the parents becomes the object of little Hans's curiosity (and that of any child), coinciding with the birth of the baby sister.

From my point of view, for the child to dare to express his curiosity, it is a condition, at least necessary, that the child does not feel accused, reprimanded, too guilty, or blamed for his feelings or fantasies. These fantasies, together with feelings, are the ones that generate most of the questions in children. At first, little Hans's father reprimanded him for his actions and jealousy. He did not address his curiosity, which did not diminish his fears (generating an environment, as I said before, not at all facilitating but rather persecuting and accusatory). *(Father: Yes, then you'd be alone with Mommy. And a good boy doesn't want that. Little **Hans:** But he has the right to think about it.)*

That his mind could harbor all feelings, including *"bad feelings,"* is what little Hans manifests to his father when he tells him, probably in a reproachful tone, that *"a good boy would not want that,"* and he replies in some way that he is allowed to think it. It also happens in the first vignette when little Hans tells his father that *having* desire is not doing or acting it. I think both comments are little Hans's attempts to get the father not to be so strict and persecutory. In the second vignette, the father somewhat tolerates little Hans's not wanting the little sister. If these *"bad"* feelings are not allowed, others will be their bearers and depositories (this is the basis of the projection and externalization). Curiously, he told the father to write it to Freud.

Thus, I would say that not only does the appetite for knowledge and curiosity (including sexual curiosity) seem inseparable from each other, but both depend on guilt (unconscious or not) and the environment. Thus, in the first vignette, the father accuses little Hans, who, in the end, ends up with more fears that are more generalized. Meanwhile, in the second vignette, by not scolding him so much, he resumes his curiosity to know how the little sister arrived a few days later. When the parents explained it to him, the fears disappeared. What changed? Perhaps the decrease in threats and accusations made him feel less guilty; therefore, his curiosity found an outlet.

Child's curiosity

If a child's curiosity is not operational or is blocked for whatever reason, the child has no chance of ascertaining or verifying that their fantasies are just that: fantasies. Hence, the importance of children playing, experimenting, and questioning. For example, if the father accuses little Hans of wanting his sister to fall and die during the bath, but then he helps to bathe his sister and determines that, besides being jealous of her, he enjoys bathing her. So, he will verify that his jealousy is not going to harm his little sister that there is an intense loving feeling towards her, and that he will calm down.

This makes it easier for the child to understand that *"childish"* fantasies do not result in harm to external reality, nor are they understood as realities. Many questions that emerge from a child's curiosity are attempts at clarification about or around his fantasies. The child becomes phobic when he has lost his curiosity, cannot access it because it is pushed aside by guilt, or is forbidden (repressed). Notice that at the end of the first vignette, little Hans has more fears because the guilt of feeling so bad forced him to project externally that evil and danger on animals. This is the defense mechanism[4] called *"projection"* (externalization). Thus, little Hans lives with the certainty that the horse is *"the bad guy"* and will bite him, so he does not go outside.

In other words, if experimentation and curiosity are blocked, the child may live his fantasies as reality. We could say then that a non-phobic person may ask (with curiosity), *"If I do this, what will happen?"* While the phobic person will affirm, *"If I do this, something bad will happen for sure"* (without curiosity, and therefore without the possibility of checking).

In a way, Freud helps the father not to be afraid to explain to his son where babies come from and to soften that strict position on bad thoughts. In general, parents believe that their children are not sufficiently prepared to receive answers, but this is not the case. The important thing is to explain things to them in a way that could be understandable to them, according to their age. Thus, parents convey that they are not frightened by the questions raised by their children.

Furthermore, at one point, little Hans tells the father to tell Professor Freud: *"But if he thinks it, it's good. Write to the professor."* This indicates that he has Freud in mind as someone who not only helps him but also his father, whom he seems to want to convince with this request. It seems he is saying to his father, *"Tell Freud, and he will make you see that you are wrong. Compare your opinion . . . Dad, I know that Freud will understand me."* For little Hans, Freud is everyone's ally. The father accepts it.

What happened to Hans? Hans, whose real name was Herbert Graf, was able to lead a normal life. He became an opera director. All the help he and his parents received made it easier for his personal development not to be blocked. Herbert Graf died in 1975.

About fantasies

All that has been described previously would be incomplete if we did not talk a little more about fantasies. Fantasies have to yield to the fact that there is an external reality that is independent and autonomous of them. Let us say that the ideal is the coexistence of internal and external reality with an awareness of independence between them. I believe that through play, the child verifies what I said before—the doll doesn't pee, the child's gun doesn't shoot, toy chickens don't lay eggs, nor do the horses bite, nor are the children as bad as we sometimes believe (including little Hans's father, who considered him bad because he was jealous). As little Hans says, having desire is not doing. That is why they accept that the gun does not shoot, etc., and at the same time, they accept their fantasies, which allow them to play.

That is the basis of creativity and play. Play reminds the child that their fantasy cannot be fully satisfied, and if they can accept it, they will play. In phobias, this independence between realities does not exist; it is lost, and they are linked—the horse will bite. External reality is not independent of internal reality; therefore, external reality lends itself to being the scenario of internal reality. Especially if fantasy, for whatever reason, is not allowed as internal reality (or curiosity is not permitted), it will migrate to external reality.[5]

Testing and experimenting allow the child to see the toy's responses and those of the people around them and conclude the results. As I said before, they learn from the internal and external world and lay the foundations for creativity and integration that are so decisive for mental health. Thus, projecting for its own sake would not be a pathological defense as long as one can be aware of how little one influences the object, the person, the animal, etc. (endowed with its independence). So, the object, person, animal, etc., does not permeate fantasy. For example, when a child plays at shooting another person, he knows that he is not *"really"* shooting the other; little Hans does not *"really"* want his little sister to die. When a projection ceases to be an experimental hypothesis and becomes a final thesis, the problems begin (the object[6] is imbued with everything bad). But for the parents, testing, questioning, and dialogue have the same antiphobic effect as for the child. This prevents the image or the idea that parents form in their child from being filled with *"negative"* fantasies deposited and projected onto the child. In other words, parents also need to attend to their curiosities concerning their children. Suffice it to remember how when adults have nightmares, we wake up saying, thank goodness it was just a nightmare.

Parents as the ultimate role models

In all of this, the role of the parents as a reference for the child in this learning process is crucial. For example, little Hans often asked his father for more explanations (which he was finally given). The lack of clarifications, the lack of tolerance, whether conscious or unconscious, or parents who permanently address the child's persecutory superego. That is, who constantly threatens him, like what happened with little Hans's parents, who withdrew all affection and care for not being a *"good and ideal"* boy, paving the way for conflicts.

When this happens, the child's fantasies are enhanced. It becomes difficult for him to learn about the independence between the external and the internal because he is almost forced to project (externalize) somehow to get rid of the *"bad feelings,"* whose existence in his mind makes him feel guilty, lacking in curiosity, threatened as I said before, to be deprived of all affection. Only projecting will protect him from the fatal destiny of not being loved or wanted so that, to the parents and himself, the child is seen as *"good"* because everything bad is outside of himself and his mind. This causes him to see the outside world as a place filled with dangers like dangerous horses; evil is outside, not in him.

In addition, I believe that everything can be complicated if realistic hues are given to fantasy. In my opinion, the fear derives from the fact that, when pursuing the *"bad"* fantasy or feeling, the child becomes very frightened because he believes that it is easy to act on these feelings, and that is why parents are so emphatic in the face of *"bad feelings."* In reality, they convey to the child that a fantasy is easily achievable and, therefore, is extremely dangerous. This gives the fantasy a tinge of possible realism, that it is attainable, which increases the need to project[7] (for example, if the child plays at shooting and the mother or father shouts forcefully at him saying, *"What are you doing?"* he may begin to doubt the harmlessness of his game). Hence, in my opinion, the importance of little Hans's comment when he clarifies to the father, *"To feel like it is not to do it."*[8] I think it was a way of telling the father not to be so scared, that what is fantasized is not so easily done, and little Hans, 5 years old, was right.

Conclusions

To conclude, if during the child's development, his mind must organize itself, and all destructive, aggressive, hostile feelings must be deposited outside (projected), demanding a state of ideal perfection from the self, the child will fall prey to fear, and from fear to abandonment. Experimenting, exercising curiosity, daring to fantasize, and engaging with parents who can tolerate that their children are not divine will prevent the children from being frightened. As Freud says:

> *[T]he loss of love, which can be seen as a continuation of the anxiety of the infant when it misses the mother . . . . If the mother has withdrawn her love . . . , the satisfaction of the child's needs is no longer certain . . . and is exposed to the most painful feelings of stress.*

I suppose the reader is wondering why I am talking about childhood phobias. The main reason is that the most significant and common difficulties I have detected in parents are, curiously enough, similar to childhood phobias. Parents can have many fears concerning their children, which can block their childish curiosity, the desire to know what is going on, and how to fix it and channel it. If, as in children, parents' curiosity is blocked, they will begin to fantasize about a *"very bad"* child or them like a very bad *"parent."* Clearing the way for greater curiosity in parents (as in children with fears) is critical. No parent is going to be correct, sensitive, empathetic, and understanding all the time, nor do they need to be. Accepting that we are doing the best we know how and can do, braving our curiosity and our inevitable limitations in times of difficulty can be an immense help. Curiosity helps our children grow, and if we give way to it, it also helps us grow.

An underlying healing factor in the therapeutic process of little Hans was knowing that he was actively present in the mind of his father (and of Freud!). Both thinking, elbow to elbow, how to solve his fears. Caruso (2020) points out that the real discomfort, the mental tragedy, is to experience how one disappears, dies, in the mind of the other. And we could point out, in contrast, that progressive well-being appears when one feels alive, validated, and considered, in the mind of another. Being acknowledged means that the child's experiences, feelings, and thoughts are recognized and admitted. It requires attentive listening, focusing, and being fully engaged with the child. When kids feel acknowledged, they cultivate self-esteem and understand that their emotions and needs matter.

And possibly, if you are reading this book, it is because your child is alive, present, in your mind, and you are actively, like the father of little Hans, like Freud himself, helping him grow.

Also, the parents' curiosity. The original title of this book, *If You Don't Know Me, Don't Invent Me,* refers to the idea that without curiosity, you cannot know the other person; you run the risk of *"inventing"* them, creating anxieties, tensions, ignorance, discrepancies, absence of dialogue, conflicts, including transgenerational ones, etc. They easily stem from, whether in the case of parents or children, the impossibility of getting to know them and assigning them an identity that may be far from fully reflecting their personality. The dissociation of the family in those moments is significant, which supposes, in most instances, entering into a vicious circle that is painful for all. And generally, all this is due to the haste and the collapse of curiosity. And flows into *"cascades of misunderstandings"* that confuse parents and children.

Enhancing the curiosity of parents is also a fundamental task of teachers, pediatricians, therapists, psychiatrists, and psychoanalysts. In addition, the more you allow yourself and your children's curiosity, the better everything will be. There is nothing that makes a child happier than his parents talking to him about life and answering his questions, even when the questions are complicated. Everything will result in greater trust between everyone and, with it, a reinforcement of *"emotional security."*

Notes

1   In my opinion, these are the first steps for the inclusion of parents in the therapeutic process.
2   Winnicott explains that the facilitator is the environment prepared by the parents, which adapts to the child's needs and personality.
3   Meaning the fears will disappear.
4   When people are faced with experiences that overwhelm them, the mind reacts in many ways to try to relieve excessive emotional

tensions and reduce their intensity. It does not imply that the problem that causes them is solved. That is why they are called *"defense mechanisms,"* not *"resolution mechanisms."* In this case, we mean relocating the threat entirely outside. It is externalization or projection. However, some mechanisms alleviate but seriously interfere with daily life.

5 By external reality, I am referring to the outside world.

6 I use the word *"object"* to refer to people, things, and animals through which the child can observe something of his that has *"migrated"* to the outside.

7 By projecting, I am referring to the externalization process.

8 Little Hans already realized that fantasy and reality are separate.

Reference list

Bion, W. R. (1962). *Aprendiendo de la experiencia*. Heinemann.

Britton, R. (1998). *Belief and imagination. Explorations in psychoanalysis*. Routledge.

Caruso, I. A. (2020). *La separación de los amantes: una fenomenología de la muerte* (3ª ed.). México: Siglo XXI Editores.

Freud, S. (1922). *Análisis de la fobia de un niño de cinco años*. Obras Completas de Sigmund Freud, Vol. 10. Ed. Amorrortu.

Furman, E. (1957). Treatment of under-fives by way of their parents. *Psychoanalytic Study of the Child*, 12:250–262.

Furman, E. (1995). Working with and through the parents. *Child Analysis: Clinical, Theoretical and Applied*, 6:21–42.

Furman, E. (1999). The impact of parental interventions. *International Journal of Psychoanalysis*, 80:172.

Hoffer, W. (1981). Infant observations and concepts relating to infancy. In M. Brierley (ed.), *Early development and education of the child*. London: Hogarth Press (1986).

Joseph, B. (1989). Defense mechanisms and phantasy in the psychological process. In M. Feldman and E. B. Spillius (eds.), *Psychic equilibrium and psychic change*. London: Routledge.

Klein, M. (1988). *Envidia y gratitud*. Barcelona: Paidós.

Klein, M. (1925). Some theoretical conclusions regarding the emotional life on the infant. In R. Money-Kyrle, B. Joseph, E. O'Shaughnessy and H. Segal (eds.), *The writings of Melanie Klein*, Vol. III. London: Hogarth Press (1975).

Piovano, B. (2004). Parenthood and parental functions as a result of the experience of parallel psychotherapy with children and parents. *International Forum of Psychoanalysis*, 13:187–200.

Wechsler, E. (2013). *Herencias: la transmisión en psicoanálisis*. Ed. Letra Viva.

Winnicott, D. W. (1960). The theory of the parent-infant relationship. In *The maturational processes and facilitating environment*. London: Hogarth Press (1965).

Chapter 18

Psychoanalysis for parents
How do we do it?[1]

Cayetano García-Castrillón Armengou

Introduction of psychoanalysis as a parenting tool

Frequently, when some parents (in a casual setting) find out what I do, they say, *"Of course, you will tell the parents what to do!"* To which I usually reply, *"As if I know!"* Others say, *"They'll be afraid of you because you'll tell them how badly they do things,"* assuming that I know the right thing to do and will act as an implacable judge against the parents. Many comments arise along these lines. I have observed that, on the one hand, they consider that, as a psychoanalyst, I possess a kind of *"special"* wisdom. On the other hand, they believe this *"wisdom"* gives me the exclusive privilege of knowing the prescriptions and definitive solutions. Nothing could be further from the truth. Each family is different, as I pointed out in the introduction; they have their own personalities, virtues, conflicts, etc. My job is to get to know them and explore together. That is why I usually answer that what I do is investigate with the parents and their children to understand what is going on and then find the best formulas and solutions together. They usually look *"surprised"* when they hear my answer. But these reactions do not bother me, and I attribute them to the fact that people do not necessarily know about psychoanalysis in the same way that I do not know about many subjects, although I imagine what they are like, with varying degrees of success.

When parents are in my office, I explain to them what we will investigate, how we will go about it, and why we will do it that way. I have found that, upon understanding my explanations regarding the format to be followed, parents have appreciated it and are reassured. I do not think it differs from what other professionals, such as

DOI: 10.4324/9781003581543-21

pediatricians, teachers, social workers, or therapists, do daily. When a patient, student, or parent knows where things are going, they feel contained.[2] Needless to say, there are many interesting TV documentaries on how things are done, so why not pass this on to the parents? That is the purpose of this chapter. Even if you, the parents, are not going to consult a professional, you can consider the importance of research and cultivate your own curiosity.[3] After all, this is another of the main objectives of this book.

Therefore, it is essential to explain the basics of setting clearly to parents and why it is done this way. It also helps to define objectives, what we seek, and what we intend. Thus, psychoanalysis is not a set of correct occurrences, psychological reflections, or brilliant conclusions. It is a way of proceeding and an attempt to find a greater and deeper understanding from which the change is viable. Explaining the setting step by step, the sequence to follow, the reasons for doing it this way, and why giving all the space to the parents and kids makes sense. It helps to establish an alliance and know as well as possible how they see the situation, what they think and understand, their insight, how they relate, and their level of desperation. Convey to parents that the psychoanalyst wonders, investigates, and rectifies, if necessary, that he gives importance to curiosity. Also, psychoanalysts do not expect to be obeyed. Without all this previous work, I believe it would be difficult to access any successful work.

Psychoanalysis for parents

All that I have written previously, I have called *"psychoanalysis for parents."* Now, I will briefly explain the methodology of psychoanalysis. We call it *"framework or setting,"* which essentially refers to the format to follow. This format is the one I explain at the beginning to the consulting parents so that they are clear about the roadmap we are going to follow and why. In other words, we will follow the roadmap to develop the best possible *navigation charts*. I clarify that this is schematic since the nuances are innumerable. Still, I think that this way, it is possible to get at least a concrete and observable idea of this method that I have been refining over the years and will continue to do so.

We have all painted our house at some point, and we know that what will determine, to a great extent, the final result will be the previous preparation, such as putting up tape, fixing minor damages, etc. The painting itself is almost the least labor-intensive part. Next, I will comment on these initial preparations or *"setting."*

But when is the right time to consult? In my opinion, when parents see that something is not right or they have doubts. All parents detect it. The worst thing, in my experience, is to rely on tired phrases such as *"he will grow out of it," "it's because of the cell phone," "it's nonsense, he just wants attention,"* or that a child is wrongly diagnosed with ADHD, etc. Otherwise, with everything described previously, parents can get a reasonably clear idea of when to consult.

In other words, avoiding *"oversimplifying"* the causality and pathogenesis[4] of conflicts in the family is important. Doing so (*oversimplifying*) has three serious consequences. The first is a degradation in clinical practice, the second is worsening the situation, and the third is fragmentation,[5] which in psychoanalysis is called *"dissociation"* and, to a more extreme degree, *"splitting."* In other words, getting in touch with reality is extremely difficult. Numerous psychologists, therapists, psychiatrists, and psychoanalysts have tried to combat this danger. Freud already pointed out that the simplification of things constitutes a severe threat to the treatment of patients; thus, in his article *"Can Laymen Practice Analysis? Dialogues with an Impartial Judge"* in 1926, he comments:

> *If I tell you something comprehensible . . . . I will present it to you as if it were a finished doctrinal edifice . . . . We have developed it gradually . . . and we modified it continually in close contact with observation, until at last it took a form in which it seems to serve our purposes.*[6]

These words are a clear manifesto against *"simplification."* In other words, there are no shortcuts to solving problematic situations. As Freud points out, close contact with observation is the most crucial aspect to strengthen when working with families; the more you observe, the better. Observing gives way to curiosity, and this gives way to experimentation, to new attempts of closeness, and frees us from the heavy demand of immediate success that stops so many processes of progression and advancement. Each attempt, even when unsuccessful,[7] brings us closer to the most fruitful knowledge, thus opening the way to perseverance, which, as we know, allows us to make possible what at first seems impossible.

Establishing a therapeutic framework

My starting point depends on various factors. While there are many, the two principal factors are age and the seriousness of the situation. Based on these, I decide who I see first: the child or the parents. If the child is already a teenager, I see them first and then the parents. If the child is a toddler, I see the parents first and then the child. The second criterion is the seriousness of the situation and the degree of anxiety of the parents. If they are very distressed, I see the parents first, regardless of the child's age. If the parents are overwhelmed, I consider it an emergency and, therefore, a priority to attend to them as soon as possible. This leads to the following possibilities:

1. When the children are adolescents or young adults, the first interview is with them and then with the parents.
2. When the children are minors, the first interview or interviews are with the parents and then with the children.
3. Indications to all parents, regardless of the age of their children.

1. When the children are teenagers or young adults, the first interview is with them and then with the parents

A.   First meeting with a young adult or adolescent

I will present the case of 21-year-old David. Despite having made an appointment with the parents because, on the phone call, I noticed they were very concerned. I told them that after talking to them, I would speak to their son, but their son came first. It was significant that they told their son to go first. When I realized this, I wondered if the parents thought that they had already tried everything and that it would be a waste of time for them to attend, and, therefore, there was no point in them coming. This was just a hypothesis.

The young man arrives very willing, anxious, and talkative. He tells me that he has not been able to study for two years and now does not know if he likes the degree he has chosen and is very stressed about it. He also does not know what he would like to study. He tells me bitterly that his parents only tell him to study and finish his degree, to be practical, even if he doesn't like it. He doesn't talk to them and they are becoming increasingly distant and have been for months. He tells me that he's sure his parents told me, on the phone call, that he is hooked on his cell phone. I told him yes, but that I didn't think they said it as a criticism but rather in a tone of concern about what could be happening with him and blocking him.

That relieved him. He tells me he had a tough breakup with his first love and that he *"sank into the well."* He didn't go out or study and was only on his cell phone. He had been cheerful, the fun one in the group, the one who had never had any problems with his studies; in short, everything was going well for him, including his relationship with his parents. He considers that he has already overcome the worst of that breakup. In fact, he has a new girlfriend. He went to therapy, where he understood that he had *"idealized"* that girl and that, in reality, things did not work with her from the beginning. He says, *"You know. You put the first girl on a pedestal, and you are blinded."* I agreed with him and commented that the work he and his previous therapist did was excellent. I also asked him why he had not returned to his previous therapist. He replied that they had reached a point where they were no longer moving forward and agreed that it would be better to look for someone else to bring other perspectives.

What is happening with him now is that he doesn't like what he is studying and doesn't know what he wants or would like to do. When I asked him about his cell phone use, he replied,

> *I don't know if I've become addicted or not. I don't use it so much anymore. But in that period, it was the only thing that allowed me to remember who I was. When I saw things, I laughed, but inside, I didn't. It was where I found myself:[8] cheerful and funny. My father was very strict with me the first year after the breakup . . . . They're hammering me about the degree.*

These were the main points. I told him that it seemed to me that his parents thought he had completely gotten over the breakup with his first girlfriend and, therefore, they only understood that not studying must be due to considerable irresponsibility and that *"corrective measures"* would fix everything.[9] Finally, I told him two things. One was that he learned to discern whether or not he might like a new girl, which is important so as not to idealize again. The second thing was that he was able to question whether he liked his career or not; perhaps he had not even considered it before, and that, in my opinion, the failure would be to deny oneself asking this question.

He replied, *"It's a lifetime working in that field, dedicating myself to a career I do not like. That is something to think about, right?"* I answered that it was *"highly advisable."*

After that, I told him I would talk to his parents and asked if he agreed. He did. I also asked if there was anything he had told me that I should be *"careful"* about. He gave me permission to talk about everything. This clearly indicated his desire to regain the good relationship that had been severed with his parents. I then explained that once I spoke with them and found out how they saw the situation, what they thought, and what they had tried, we would all talk again. He agreed.

As I commented in the chapter on adolescents, the importance of first love is worth noting. They really are critical and complex moments from the emotional point of view because, above all, both men and women experience them as personal and total validation.

As you can see, I observed the following steps:

1. Listen to what happened to him.
2. Give my opinion and the hypothesis of what I have understood about what could have happened and what could still happen.
3. Describe what the next steps will be. Meet with the parents and then with all three of them and determine what to do, why, and what for.

Let me also explain why I thought David might have always been insecure and afraid to make decisions. Perhaps he has always felt that getting things wrong could be catastrophic. I thought this, but I didn't tell him at the time; instead, I waited to check as I got to know him better whether all this was true or not. This impression occurred to me because of what he told me about idealizing his first girlfriend.

If we stop to think a little, we can idealize many things or people. We can idealize an ideology, a career, a person, a therapist, etc.[10] But how does idealization work?[11] In reality, there is a search to eliminate any insecurity so that one is already *"totally"* sure that one is not wrong and does not have to look for anything else. Thus, it prevents (apparently) one's fears about the possibility of being wrong. Especially if making a mistake is experienced, as I said before, in a catastrophic and dramatic way. That is why it is imperative in parenting to de-dramatize mistakes and consider them as a natural part of development.

This framework is the one I follow if I see the children first. Then, when I see the parents, I will observe what they agree or disagree with about what their child said, checking if, in some way, they have also detected what I have suspected, as I mentioned before, etc.

I can tell you that I find the enormous similarity between what parents and children say surprising, even when there is a great distance between them, similarities that usually have not been detected.

B. First meeting with the parents of young adults and adolescents

Next, I will describe the guidelines I follow with the parents. Then, as an illustration, I will comment on the interview with the young man's parents from the previous section.

Evidently, the fact that they have taken the difficult step of coming to the consultation implies their desire and need for help. Typically, they tell me they have tried everything and not obtained results. Indeed, they have tried everything they could. I try to make them understand that it can be a great help not to be crushed by guilt, helplessness, or excessive blame for the child, themselves, or each other. Parents, with help, can be *"of great help"* in the way of becoming closer and having a more communicative attitude with their children. Improving communication will be the first great objective to pursue, more than changes in the child. This is key since it is the basis for possible changes, and this is how I explain it to the parents: *"Our first and definitive common objective is to improve dialogue; only from there will we have real possibilities of change."* But sometimes they don't talk to each other, as is happening with David, and my presence can be the one that channels the dialogue. Typically, this is how it is restored later at home, little by little.

Also, based on what they have explained to me, my proposal is as follows:

a. To make a provisional, dynamic clinical assessment, considering that new elements may appear later will make us revise the initial diagnosis. This allows parents to identify that they face a problem with a name. As I've noted, parents formulate their own diagnosis of the situation.

b. Make a prognosis according to existing favorable and unfavorable indicators.

c. If I see that it is necessary, I carry out an uninterrupted work plan as long as needed. It is usually a weekly or biweekly meeting of approximately one hour in which the parents report, give their opinions, ask questions, etc. For my part, I will offer them my interpretation and other ways of understanding the situation while expressing my doubts. I will ask questions that allow me to understand them better or open an array of information on aspects they may have overlooked, and I will also advise them on how to react in moments of great intensity at home. In other words, how to manage the family imbalance while trying to detect which situations may have produced it, which I call triggers or *"trigger moments."* It seems complex, but they are usually the same. So, the parents and I will attempt to understand fully *"what happens behind the scenes,"* or the emotional background behind human behavior.

I also warn them that it is normal that, at the beginning, parents are at odds and blame each other for the poor progress. And I make it clear that this will not lead anywhere, as I explained before.

d. Give them some initial recommendations.

Let's see how the interview with David's parents went:

Upon entering the room and after the appropriate customary greetings, they sit on the couch. After momentary silence and uncertainty, I asked them if they wanted to start or if it would be better for me to do it. This relaxed them. They tell me that they are very worried. Immediately, the father says that he has been very practical in life and has told his son to finish his studies and that then, if he does not like it, he can do something else afterward. However, he does not know if he was wrong or not. They comment that no matter how much they tell their son to study, he doesn't get started. The mother says that her son tells them one thing, but it turns out not to be true. For example, he says he has gone to take an exam, but then it turns out not to be the case. They recognize that the breakup with the first love of his life was a very hard *"blow."*

They tell me, *"No matter how much we insist and tell him that he is putting everything in danger, including his future, he does not react."* At this point in the interview, they seemed frightened and overwhelmed by the situation, not parents who deeply resent their son. They tell me they want him to be the same as before, but there is no way, and that they are struck by the fact that everyone outside the home says he is friendly, funny, and talkative. Verbatim, they said, *"We don't see this son at home. He goes into his room, eats separately, doesn't want us to talk to him, tells us that we don't help him and that he hates us. "* He also has a new girlfriend who is nothing like the previous one, which he now realizes was toxic.

At this point, I already had an idea of the situation. The parents assumed that he was over the emotional wounds of the breakup, but in my opinion, he must still be very insecure. The mother agreed that she also saw him as insecure.

I added that being able to date another girl was a big step forward because the disappointments of first loves are very complex because young men feel they are either being approved or not. They agreed with that, also. I explained to them what I told their son about the cell phone, that it was a way of rescuing himself. Thus, the starting point was rock bottom, a place from which he had not yet fully emerged, although he had made much progress. In addition, as I told their son, I told them that in the same way he can now think and reflect on whether he likes his new partner, he must conclude that it is also advisable to ask himself that question regarding his studies. I said their son is afraid not to ask the question, and they do not want him to ask it because they also, like their son, want to see the person from before. They understand that the son from before will come through his studies and grades and, with him, normality. Interestingly, the son did it with the cell phone. He clung to the cell phone to feel like before, and the parents clung to his studies to see the son from before. In different ways, they all wanted the old one.

2. When the children are minors, the first interview or interviews are with the parents and then the children

As I explained earlier, if the children are minors, I begin to do ongoing work with the parents and delay for a while, if possible, before talking to their children. The main reason is to give the parents time to understand what may be going on and give them a better insight into the situation so that they can initiate new avenues of approach and emotional management with their children. This strategy also allows me to see what changes may or may not occur in their children and family dynamics. A child's adaptability is much greater than that of an adolescent or young adult. What I have found surprising about this way of proceeding is that frequently, the children no longer need to go to therapy and that well-established, long-lasting changes take place in the family. In the following, I will explain the fundamental basis of this approach.

In these first interviews as always, parents must convey the following to the son or daughter: *"We have gone to a professional to advise us on how to improve communication with you."* That message shows the child that you are mobilized for that purpose. It makes it clear that you are not coming to complain about them or say, *"how bad our son or daughter is,"* but to find a space for reflection, not for complaint space for understanding. I repeat, this is vital.

I tell parents I will want to know their son's or daughter's opinion on our work's evolution, *"just their opinion,"* when I consider it time. In the beginning, I ask via the parents, and when we've been going for a while, I invite the child to come in. Often, this invitation is not necessary because it is they who want to come and tell their point of view and version of the situation. As an anecdote, I remember a 10-year-old boy who said, verbatim, to his parents: *"When can I talk to the boss?"*

Of course, I tell the parents to inform the child that they can come and talk to me alone under the usual conditions of confidentiality.[12] Usual means that everything is confidential, except for what puts the child's life or the lives of others at risk. I clarify this to the parents or the child when we talk. All the children have understood this, and if they need therapy, I tell them and explain the reasons, whether they take my advice or not. But the important thing is that they are always welcome to come and talk to me, the parents, or both of us.

I also consider this point decisive because, generally, when a child, or even the parents, has difficulties, the usual tendency is to resort to the punitive route in its different versions to try to solve the problems, which never work. With the permanent invitation to the children, I intend two things:

1. The first is to show them (and the parents as well) that their opinion is valid and that therapy is not a *"criminal prosecution"* either for the children or for the parents but an attempt to see how things could change, which requires everyone's participation, contributions, and ideas. So that by testing, trying, and working *"as a team,"* we can all make progress together.
2. Conveying that therapy is not a means of judgment will allow them to get used to the idea so that, in case they need it (as is often the case), they can approach it with less fear. In other words, it paves

the way. In psychoanalytical terms, it would correlate to diminishing the highly elevated paranoid anxieties that tend to exist in situations of family conflicts.

This structuring also lets me make it clear to parents that there is no magic formula that solves everything if we follow it. I tell them that the prescriptions will come to us by thinking them over, seeing what advantages they have and what we are looking for by using them, and that we will constantly and continually evaluate their usefulness or lack of usefulness. This makes it easier for the parents to come up with beneficial ideas, which are usually the ones that work best, through trial and error and review. This, in turn, allows parents not to fall into pits of despair when something fails or doesn't work.

The next step: Interviewing the children

After some time working with the parents, I usually talk to their child. My approach is to tell them how I see their parents, what idea I have of them, and where I observe their difficulties and abilities so that they get a very clear idea of how I have gotten to know them. I also tell them what the parents tell me about their children, what worries them, if they see them suffering, etc. This allows me to ask them if they see what I do. Many times, they say yes, or they add different aspects. I also clarify what I am trying to achieve with the parents. For example, I tell them, *"You may have noticed that your parents are asking you more questions than before, and that's because we've talked about how that might be interesting, that they're looking for your point of view."* And I add, *"Do you think what we've been working on is doing any good?"*

This brief example illustrates the climate of dialogue that I intend to establish with the children, where thinking over, seeing what works and what doesn't, listening to their opinions, and my willingness to allow them to question our work are central points.

I also explain to them what idea I have formed of them. For example: *"From what your parents told me about you, I imagine you are . . . is that so?"* At this point, the kids are usually quite open because they have already realized this is not about blaming anyone. Then, it's easier to talk about whether they think they're having any difficulties or whether I think they might be and, from there, make the necessary suggestions.

I do not know what other colleagues' experience is, but I find it very curious that, on countless occasions, adolescents are more understanding of their parents than they seem to be. It is very common for them to tell me, *"I understand why they are angry with me,"* to which I usually reply, *"Have you told them?"* And they typically say no, to which I respond that it wouldn't hurt.

It isn't easy to express the wide range of situations, emotional reactions, psychological defenses, counter-identifications with the parents, countertransference reactions, etc., that unfold in these sessions. But we should be attentive to all of them.

3. Recommendations to all parents, regardless of their children's age

1. Provide parents with an immediate means of contact in case they need help at a specific moment between visits.
2. In case of seriousness, explain the channels to which they can resort: medical emergency rooms, psychiatric emergency treatment, etc., when the shared work cannot cover everything or situations exceed capacity. Sometimes, it is also necessary because the time needed to restructure the family functioning is longer than the events unfolding in real time. It is essential to keep this time lag in mind from a practical and technical point of view.
3. To enhance the parents' capacity for observation and detection concerning their children (and vice versa) or the progress of the process, it is imperative to point out any change in how they relate to each other. For example, they can talk longer without arguing or yelling at home is reduced.
4. The basic premise is not to mock or belittle the other.
5. Obviously, the possibility of talking to teachers or the school can be of great help, and sometimes it is decisive. In general, teachers are very, very helpful.
6. The process and development of the work. All anxieties and concerns deserve time and analysis. As I pointed out at the beginning, each family is unique and genuine. But in general, several aspects tend to come to the fore. I keep these aspects[13] very present in the interviews with parents, and in one way or another, when I discover how they develop, I explain it to the parents:

   a. The upbringing and relationship styles that the parents experienced in their upbringing. As I pointed out in the previous chapter on *"Transmission,"* the tendency to repeat them is widespread; after all, our parents are our primary reference for all of us.

b. Parents' fears concerning their children. Taking this aspect into account is critical.

c. What each family understands as *"the forms of resolution."*

d. The psychopathological aspects that derive from the projection of one's conflicts on the other are usually very present. (For example, when a parent is excessively demanding of his child, from whom he expects submission. Their demands end up being *"heaped"* on their child, and the situation can become blocked.)

7. After the full initial assessment, always give the parents as complete *"feedback"* as possible.

For example, I will show you the *"feedback"* I gave David's parents. In short:

a. It was useless to pressure him because it generated a constant climate of tension and mutual suspicion, feelings that the situation was catastrophic and that the only and definitive solution was to study.

b. The following were indicators of a good prognosis: their son's emotional recovery after the breakup of his *"platonic love"* relationship; his open and sincere way of talking to me and his allowing me to use everything he told me to speak to them; the desire to know what he would like to study or not study without a clear objective.

c. I understood that searching for what he would genuinely like to study was an extension of learning and that it is not advisable to go through life unthinkingly. That is to say, it was a positive side effect after going through the breakup with his platonic love and how idealization can cause one to be blind. However, it also blinds us to study something by *"inertia"* without further thought. I also commented that the search had not yet been completed, although their son understood that they would all like him to know already what he wants. After making this point, the mother commented, *"I ask him to tell me what he likes. He tells me that he doesn't know, and we get stuck there."* I responded that in my observation, with so much worry that everything had been lost, the idea of investigating and searching had been left out of total consideration.

d. All of the preceding made me optimistic. Also, in principle, I did not consider using the cell phone as a problem since it has not been established as the only means of *"relief"* and was only transitory.[14]

e. I proposed that I meet with their son regularly and, in the meantime, continue talking all together (or separately, as we saw fit) as openly as possible. I suggested they think about it and said there was no problem talking to their son about all this because David would surely be expectant after our interview and our conclusions.

f. Finally, I said I would call him to set up another appointment and that we would continue talking to evaluate how everything was going. The parents agreed with this *"road map."*

Final comment

To conclude, I must emphasize that, while it is true that, inevitably, all parents make mistakes because they are not perfect, it is also true, as I pointed out before, that *"they also make many good decisions"* and are, or can be, of great help, more than they may think at first. It is very striking to observe how children excuse their parents' mistakes when they see that they are trying to change, and if the atmosphere calms down, children also try to take care of their parents. If affection, positive appraisal, and kindness are present in addition to everything discussed so far, things will improve sooner or later.

I hope I have managed to convey some ideas that may be useful and illuminating for you and that you will not be alarmed if you recognize any aspect that you consider could be improved. We are not born *"knowing the right answer"* but can learn, rectify, and grow. Also, consider your own innumerable successes that benefit your children and your children's efforts to advance. So, I hope that a few of these misunderstandings have been *"cleared up"* with the help of your curiosity and desire to understand and challenge distress and the unknown.

Finally, I encourage you to question the professionals openly. This is not to disavow us, nor will we be upset about it. On the contrary, it will help us considerably to do more and better research. I hope you will have this critical and constructive spirit toward everything expressed in the book, and as I pointed out at the beginning, understand the book as a suggestion and not as *"the definitive."*

I will be glad if I have succeeded in awakening new questions and bringing you some understanding. I sincerely appreciate your interest. Good luck, and enjoy your kids. You are probably doing much better than you think you are.

Thank you.

Notes

1 Technical considerations of this method of parental assistance.
2 When a baby is born, the experience of seeing that its parents receive, perceive, respond, and react to their feelings, discomfort, joy, etc., is fundamental. Feeling and experiencing that the parents are there generates enormous emotional tranquility and security in the baby. This process is called containment, which we will value throughout life. In their work, therapists, pediatricians, and teachers also transmit this same disposition towards parents and regenerate the experience of containment. Thus strengthening the bond, security, trust, and the idea that they are not *"alone"* in the face of problems.
3 Curiosity that, as I have pointed out previously, usually collapses in times of conflict or family difficulties.
4 In medicine, pathogenesis means the processes that are generated and triggered by a cause.
5 Fragmentation in psychoanalysis refers to only contemplating a *"part or fragment"* of the problem or its causes, excluding many other essential ones. It is like finishing a puzzle without putting all the pieces together. Dissociation and splitting refer to degrees of fragmentation. Dissociation is to fragment relatively little, and splitting is to fragment significantly. That is why fragmentation, by eliminating *"pieces,"* makes us think in a weak, biased, and simplified way.
6 Freud also concludes that: "*I certainly cannot guarantee that its present expression will be the definitive one. You know that science is no surprise; it lacks the characters of immutability, precision, and perpetuity so longed for by human thought.*"
7 We are reminded of a famous quote from Edison: *"I have not failed; I discovered 999 ways not to make a light bulb."*
8 I found his comment very striking. He clearly used his cell phone as an antidepressant to keep from sinking to the bottom.
9 Let's remember what I talked about earlier: how action-reaction generates magical solutions that create the fantasy that everything will be fixed all at once.

10 The most common form of idealization of the therapist is to consider that they know everything and thus generate a false security that everything will go well as long as everything the therapist says is *"done."* This generates a dangerous child-like dependency.

11 Political or religious leaders can also be idealized under the fantasy of protection and security. This facilitates polarization and the development of extremism.

12 I also make that point with adolescents and young adults.

13 Based on these points, each process is particular, and this is the work to be conducted.

14 However, on other occasions, cell phone use is solidified as the only and primary means of relief. In these cases, it does pose a serious problem.

Reference list

Alexander, F. (1935). The problem of psychoanalytic technique. *Psychoanalytic Quarterly*, 4:588.

Bion, W. R. (1961). *Experiences in groups: And other papers*. Routledge.

Bleger, J. (1966). Psychoanalysis of the psychoanalytic frame. *International Journal of Psychoanalysis*, 48:511–519.

Britton, R. (2004). Subjectivity, objectivity, and triangular space. *The Psychoanalytic Quarterly*, 73:47–61.

Farber, B. A., and Nevas, D. (2001). Parents' perceptions of the effects of their child's therapy. *Journal of the American Academy of Psychoanalysis and Dynamic Psychiatry*, 29(2), 319–330.

Ferenzi, S. (1928–33). *Contributions to the Problems and Methods of Psychoanalysis*. London: Hogarth Press (1955).

Fonagy, P., and Target, M. (1996). Predictors of outcome in child psychoanalysis: A retrospective study of 763 cases at the Anna Freud Center. *Journal of the American Psychoanalytic Association*, 44:27–73.

Freud, S. (1911–13). *Trabajos sobre técnica psicoanalítica y otras obras*, Vol. 12. Ed. Amorrortu.

Freud, S. (1913). On beginning the treatment. In *The standard edition of the complete works of Sigmund Freud*, Vol. XII. London: Hogarth Press (1950–74).

Freud, S. (1926). *¿Pueden los legos ejercer el análisis? Diálogos con un juez imparcial*. Obras Completas, Vol. XX. Amorrortu Editores.

Freud, S. (1937). *Construcciones en psicoanálisis*. Obras Completas de Sigmund Freud, Vol. 23. Ed. Amorrortu.

Furman, E. (1995). Working with and through the parents. *Child Analysis: Clinical, Theoretical and Applied*, 6:21–42.

Furman, E. (1999). The impact of parental interventions. *International Journal of Psychoanalysis*, 80:172.

García-Castrillón, C. (2007). *Ser padres, ¿una misión imposible?* Ed. Glosa.

Icart, A., and Freixas, J. (2013). *La familia: Comprensión dinámica e intervenciones terapéuticas*. Ed. Herder.

Mannoni, M. (1974). *El Niño, su Enfermedad y los Otros*. Tel-Aviv: Am Oved.

Meltzer, D. (1975). Adhesive identification. *Contemporary Psychoanalysis*, 11:289.

Novick, K. K., and Novick, J. (2005). *Working with parents makes therapy work*. Aronson.

Piovano, B. (2003). Comentario sobre "Psicoterapia padre-hijo y tratamiento psicoanalítico: ¿contradicción o inspiración mutua?" de Christiane Ludwig-Körne. *Foro Internacional de Psicoanálisis*, 12:259–264.

Slade, A. (2005). Parental reflective functioning: An introduction. *Attachment & Human Development*, 7:269–281.

Torras, E. (2012). *Normalidad, psicopatología y tratamientos en niños, adolescentes y familias*. Barcelona: Ed. Octaedro.

Winnicott, D. W. (1965). *Maturation processes and the facilitating environment*. International University Press.

Bibliography

Aberastury, A., and Knobel, M. (1984). *La adolescencia normal. Un enfoque psicoanalítico.* Paidos.

Alexander, F. (1935). The problem of psychoanalytic technique. *Psychoanalytic Quarterly*, 4:588.

Balint, M. (1952). Early developmental stages of the ego. In *Primary love and psycho-analytic technique.* London: Hogarth Press (1973).

Balint, M. (1963). On being empty of oneself. *The International Journal of Psychoanalysis*, 44:470.

Balint, M. (1968). *The basic fault.* London: Tavistock Publications.

Balint, M. (1969). Trauma and object relationship. *The International Journal of Psychoanalysis*, 50:429.

Bertolini, R., and Nissim, S. (2002). Video games and children's imagination. *Journal of Child Psychotherapy*, 28(3):305–325.

Bick, E. (1962). Symposium on child analysis: Child analysis today. *International Journal of Psychoanalysis*, 43:328–32.

Bick, E., and Harris, M. (2018). *The Tavistock model: Collected papers of Martha Harris and Esther Bick.* Karnac Books.

Bion, W. (1959). Attacks on linking. *The International Journal of Psychoanalysis*, 40:308–315.

Bion, W. R. (1961). *Experiences in groups: And other papers.* Routledge.

Bion, W. R. (1962). *Learning from experience.* Maresfield Reprints, London: Karnac Books (1984).

Bleger, J. (1966). Psychoanalysis of the psychoanalytic frame. *International Journal of Psychoanalysis*, 48:511–519.

Blum, H. P. (2004). Separation-individuation theory and attachment theory. *Journal of the American Psychoanalytic Association*, 52(2):535–553.

Britton, R. (1998a). *Belief and imagination. Explorations in psychoanalysis.* Routledge.

Britton, R. (1998b). Subjectivity, objectivity, and potential space. In *Belief and imagination*. Routledge.

Britton, R. (2004). Subjectivity, objectivity, and triangular space. *Psychoanalytic Quarterly*, 73:47–61.

Fairbairn, W. (1946). Object-relationships and dynamic structure. *The International Journal of Psychoanalysis*, 27:30.

Farber, B. A., and Nevas, D. (2001). Parents' perceptions of the effects of their child's therapy. *Journal of the American Academy of Psychoanalysis and Dynamic Psychiatry*, 29(2), 319–330.

Ferenczi, S. (1926). *The problem of acceptance of unpleasant ideas in advances knowledge of the sense of reality*. Further contributions. London: Karnac Books (1980).

Ferenzi, S. (1933). Relaxation and education. In *Final contributions to problems and the methods of psychoanalysis*. London: Hogarth Press (1955).

Fernando, J. (2002). El sentimiento de culpa prestado. In *Libro anual de psicoanálisis XVI*. São Paulo-Brasil: Ed. Escuta Ltda.

Fonagy, P., and Target, M. (1996). Predictors of outcome in child psychoanalysis: A retrospective study of 763 cases at the Anna Freud Center. *Journal of the American Psychoanalytic Association*, 44:27–73.

Fonagy, P., and Target, M. (2002). Jugando con la realidad III. In *Libro anual de psicoanálisis XVI*. São Paulo-Brasil: Ed. Escuta Ltda.

Freud, S. (1904). The psychopathology of everyday life. In *The standard edition of the complete works of Sigmund Freud*, Vol. VI. London: Hogarth Press (1950–74).

Freud, S. (1911). Formulations on the two principles of mental functioning. In *The standard edition of the complete works of Sigmund Freud*, Vol. XII. London: Hogarth Press (1950–74).

Freud, S. (1911–13). *Trabajos sobre técnica psicoanalítica y otras obras*, Vol. 12. Ed. Amorrortu.

Freud, S. (1913). On beginning the treatment. In *The standard edition of the complete works of Sigmund Freud*, Vol. XII. London: Hogarth Press (1950–74).

Freud, S. (1915). *Consideraciones de actualidad sobre la guerra y la muerte*. Obras Completas, Vol. VI. Amorrortu Editores.

Freud, S. (1920). *Más allá del principio del placer*. Obras Completas de Sigmund Freud, Vol. 18. Ed. Amorrortu.

Freud, S. (1922). *Análisis de la fobia de un niño de cinco años*. Obras Completas de Sigmund Freud, Vol. 10. Ed. Amorrortu.

Freud, S. (1926). *¿Pueden los legos ejercer el análisis? Diálogos con un juez imparcial*. Obras Completas, Vol. XX. Ed. Amorrortu.

Freud, S. (1927). The future of an illusion. In *The standard edition of the complete works of Sigmund Freud*, Vol. XXI. London: Hogarth Press (1950–74).

Freud, S. (1937). Constructions in analysis. In *The standard edition of the complete works of Sigmund Freud*, Vol. XXIII. London: Hogarth Press (1950–74).

Freud, S. (1937). *Construcciones en psicoanálisis*. Obras Completas de Sigmund Freud, Vol. 23. Ed. Amorrortu.

Furman, E. (1957). Treatment of under-fives by way of their parents. *Psychoanalytic Study of the Child*, 12:250–262.

Furman, E. (1995). Working with and through the parents. *Child Analysis: Clinical, Theoretical and Applied*, 6:21–42.

Furman, E. (1999). The impact of parental interventions. *International Journal of Psychoanalysis*, 80:172.

Garcia-Castrillón, C. (2007). *Ser padres, ¿una misión imposible?* Ed. Glosa.

Harris, M. (1983). *Se hijo de 12 a 14 años*. Paidos.

Hinshelwood, H. D. (1989). *Diccionario del Pensamiento Kleiniano*. Amorrortu Editores.

Hoffer, W. (1981). Infant observations and concepts relating to infancy. In M. Brierley (ed.), *Early development and education of the child*. London: Hogarth Press (1986).

Horney, K. (1936). The problem of the negative therapeutic reaction. *Psychoanalytic Quarterly*, 5:29–44.

Icart, A., and Freixas, J. (2013). *La familia: Comprensión dinámica e intervenciones terapéuticas*. Ed. Herder.

Icart, A., and Freixas, J. (2020). *A mí no me pasa nada*. Octaedro.

Isaacs, S. (1952). The nature and function of phantasy. In M. Klein, P. Heimann, S. Isaacs and J. Riviere (eds.), *Developments in psycho-analysis*. London: Hogarth Press (1970).

Jacobs, L. (ed.). (n.d.). *Parent-centered child therapy: Attachment, identification, and reflective functions*. Lanham, MD: Jason Aronson.

Joseph, B. (1989). Defense mechanisms and phantasy in the psychological process. In M. Feldman and E. B. Spillius (eds.), *Psychic equilibrium and psychic change*. London: Routledge.

Kashdan, T. B., McKnight, P. E., Fincham, F. D., and Rose, P. (2011). When curiosity breeds intimacy: Taking advantage of intimacy opportunities and transforming boring conversations. *Journal of Personality*, 79(6):1067–1099.

Klein, M. (1925). Some theoretical conclusions regarding the emotional life of the infant. In R. Money-Kyrle, B. Joseph, E. O'Shaughnessy and H. Segal (eds.), *The writings of Melanie Klein*, Vol. III. London: Hogarth Press (1975).

Klein, M. (1952). On observing the behavior of young infants. In R. Money-Kyrle, B. Joseph, E. O'Shaughnessy and H. Segal (eds.), *The writings of Melanie Klein*, Vol. III. London: Hogarth Press (1975).

Klein, M. (1988). *Envidia y gratitud*. Barcelona: Paidós.

Lassers, E., and Lassers, W. J. (1985). Children and parents in the divorce court. *American Journal of Psychoanalysis*, 45:77–79.

Lingiardi, V., and McWilliams, N. (2017). *Psychodynamic diagnostic manual*, 2nd Edition. Guilford.

Malberg, N. T. (2015). Activating mentalization in parents: An integrative framework. *Journal of Infant, Child & Adolescent Psychotherapy*, 14:232–245.

Mannoni, M. (1974). *El Niño, su Enfermedad y los Otros*. Tel-Aviv: Am Oved.

Meltzer, D. (1975). Adhesive identification. *Contemporary Psychoanalysis*, 11:289.

Morgan, M. (2020). Being a couple and developing the capacity for creative parenting: A psychoanalytic perspective. *Journal of Child Psychotherapy*, 46:191–205.

Novick, K., and Novick, J. (2019). *Trabajo con padres y terapia con hijos*. Ed. Herder.

Novick, K. K., and Novick, J. (2005). *Working with parents makes therapy work*. Aronson.

Pichon Rivière, A. A. (1957). La inclusión de los padres en el cuadro de la situación analítica y el manejo de esta situación a través de la interpretación. *Revista de Psicoanálisis (REVAPA)*, 14:137–146.

Piovano, B. (2003). Comentario sobre "Psicoterapia padre-hijo y tratamiento psicoanalítico: ¿contradicción o inspiración mutua?" *Foro Internacional de Psicoanálisis*, 12:259–264.

Piovano, B. (2004). Parenthood and parental functions as a result of the experience of parallel psychotherapy with children and parents. *International Forum of Psychoanalysis*, 13:187–200.

Sandler, J. (1967). Trauma, strain and development. In S. S. Furst (ed.), *Psychic trauma*. New York and London: Basic Books.

Sandler, J. (2002). Acerca de la comunicación del paciente al analista: no todo es identificación proyectiva. In *Libro anual de psicoanálisis*, Vol. XVI. São Paulo-Brasil: Ed. Escuta Ltda.

Schoffer, D. (2008). *La Función Paterna en la Clínica Freudiana*. Lugar Editorial.

Schultheis, A. M., Mayes, L. C., and Rutherford, H. J. V. (2019). Associations between emotion regulation and parental reflective functioning. *Journal of Child and Family Studies*, 28:1094–1104.

Segal, H. (1982). *Introducción a la obra de Melanie Klein*. Paidos.

Segal, H. (1994). Phantasy and reality. *The International Journal of Psychoanalysis*, 75(2):395–401.

Slade, A. (2005). Parental reflective functioning: An introduction. *Attachment & Human Development*, 7:269–281.

Spitz, R. (1965). *The first year of life*. New York, NY: International University Press.

Steiner, J. (1997). *Refugios Psíquicos*. Biblioteca Nueva.

Sugarman, A. (2017). The transitional phenomena functions of smartphones for adolescents. *Psychoanalytic Study of the Child*, 70:135–150.

Torras, E. (2012). *Normalidad, psicopatología y tratamientos en niños, adolescentes y familia*. Barcelona: Ed. Octaedro.

Wachs, C., and Jacobs, L. (2006). Introduction. In *Parent-focused child therapy: Attachment, identification, and reflective functions*. Ed. Jason Aronson. Inc.

Wechsler, E. (2011). La transmisión del Psicoanálisis. Teoría de la técnica de las entrevistas preliminares y de la supervisión. *Revista de Psicoanálisis (APM. Asociación Psicoanalítica de Madrid)*, 63:158–170.

Wechsler, E. (2013). *Herencias: la transmisión en psicoanálisis*. Ed. Letra Viva.

Weisse, E. (1960). *The structure and dynamics of the human mind*. New York: Grune & Stratton.

Winnicott, D. (1951). Transitional objects and transitional phenomena. In *Through pediatrics to psychoanalysis*. London: Hogarth Press (1987).

Winnicott, D. (1953). Transitional objects and transitional phenomena—A study of the first not-me possession. *The International Journal of Psychoanalysis*, 34:89.

Winnicott, D. (1958). The capacity to be alone. *The International Journal of Psychoanalysis*, 39:416.

Winnicott, D. (1965a). *Los procesos de maduración y el ambiente facilitador*. Buenos Aires: Paidós.

Winnicott, D. (1965b). *Maturation processes and the facilitating environment*. International University Press.

Winnicott, D. W. (1960). The theory of the parent-infant relationship. In *The maturational processes and facilitating environment*. London: Hogarth Press (1965).

Index

For Product Safety Concerns and Information please contact our EU
representative GPSR@taylorandfrancis.com
Taylor & Francis Verlag GmbH, Kaufingerstraße 24, 80331 München, Germany